Back on Track in 2022

by

Mike Priestley

Published in the United Kingdom
by Michael G Priestley Books.

A CIP record of this book is available from the British Library.

First printed August 2022.

Layout and design by Unwin Print, Farnsfield, Newark, Notts.
NG22 8JN.

ISBN 9780957413467

Contents

For Felix, Felicity, Gylfi, Arthur, Finn and Theodore

1. Love of Place

We all have our favourite places. We prick up our ears when we hear them mentioned by others. We may even think of them as ours - special for us in a way that others won't necessarily recognise. The picture we have of them in our minds is no doubt the result of previous visits but then filtered through our selective memory stores. Some particular details will stand out. It might be when we went, who we were with, what we did, what the weather was like or what pop song was playing at the time on our portable transistor radio.

My own love of place began on childhood family holidays, staying with relations in Winchester and Alderley Edge and then rural Shropshire and Leicestershire. They provide some of my earliest memories of anything at all. I know where I was when things happened - listening to a military band, watching steam hauled expresses go by from the top of a playground slide, marching my mum for miles under a hot sun to a way-side branch line halt in a futile attempt to see trains that never came, and throwing up in my pushchair after an illicit binge of chocolate drops washed down with a few swigs from a bottle of glycerine, both scoffed while hiding under a bed.

Later on, I became mesmerised by the view across Derwentwater to Skiddaw from our guest house in Borrowdale - the way the lighting and cloud cover changed from day to day and even from hour to hour. I had never seen mountain ranges before. I was equally struck - though much more recently - by a first view of the North West Highlands looking north along the coast from the beach at the wonderfully named Mellon Udrigle.

On a summer Sunday evening in 1965, I had cycled from a Somerset farmhouse to a nearby level crossing in the hope of photographing one of the soon to be displaced Southern Region's West Country Light Pacifics on a Cardiff to Brighton service. The light was already fading when the signalman confirmed that it was steam-hauled, but running late. Eventually the block bell rang followed by a distant whistle. It was asking too much of my modestly priced camera to do justice to No. 34005 Barnstaple under those circumstances, but the place has remained special for me ever since. I even went back in modern times. The track has long been singled, the crossing gates, semaphore signals and signalbox have all gone but the comforting memory of the moment lives on totally undimmed.

The urge to travel to new places grew. I pored over maps of the railway network and those hefty timetables in their regional colours. I read through the lists of unlikely station names from unfamiliar parts of the country - Brymbo, Strata Florida and Vulcan Halt, and I marvelled at the magic that they hinted at. Geography at school helped. I needed to know where places were and how I could get there. Eventually, we hostelled our way around Britain and Europe. Then we pretended to be a married couple to benefit fully from bed and breakfast accommodation. When our children arrived, we carted them around all over the place, though still aiming in the most part for mountains and coast. After the children had left home, we carried on as before into retirement. Then Covid 19 arrived and our lifestyle came to an abrupt halt, as it did for almost everyone else.

This book is about getting back on track, beginning with the gradual lifting of Coronavirus restrictions in the spring and summer of 2021. The time had come to recover a degree of lost confidence and put some faith in the mass vaccination process as we moved towards 2022. I was looking forward to re-acquainting myself with some of the places that were already important to me and discovering one or two others that were on my "to do" list. It seemed sensible to start local and take short journeys. The car offered protection from infection in the way that the train did not, so initially I planned to drive to a convenient railhead close to my eventual destination and take a relatively brief rail trip.

That would also introduce me to some stations that I would previously have missed seeing, up close.

The train is so much more leisurely an experience compared to navigating by-passes, double mini-roundabouts, countless traffic lights and forests of unfamiliar street signs when approaching a town by road. Is that first glimpse of a church spire through the trees the clue to the centre of town? The brakes are applied and leafy outer suburbs and retail parks give way to old industrial premises and rows of terraces. Branch lines close in at junctions and we rattle across the points, sail over and dip under road bridges and plunge through short tunnels. The oldest buildings appear and alongside them some of the most recent. High-rise developments loom over us, momentarily cutting out the light. Our stop is announced, a moment that never ceases to excite me. A day of adventure beckons. When we are travelling together, the first port of call has often been the information centre, then drip some coffee over the newly acquired freebies spread out over the table in the nearest cafe. Just what have we got to look at here and where should we start? If I'm travelling alone, however, I may not be able to prise myself very far away from the station. Well, one thing has changed for certain as a result of all this. After a gap of nearly two years, I will never take any of it for granted in quite the same way. Oh, and maybe I'll cut out the café to start with and take a picnic until things settle down a bit.

2. Doncaster

I dusted off my seriously underused, 3-year senior railcard and drove to Retford. It was time to stop cowering from Covid. I hadn't been on a train since the pandemic began, and though time normally spent on the computer or on my bike meant that lockdowns did not have nearly the same impact for me as they did for some, I had also started to feel that I was becoming institutionalised in my own home, as a result of my largely self-imposed caution about re-joining society at large. The Government's online Coronavirus dashboard showed that on the 5th of August 2021, there were 30,215 new infections recorded within the previous 24 hours and the number of people receiving hospital treatment for Covid 19 was 5,686, so it hasn't exactly gone away.

Street parking is easier at Retford (19 miles and 30 minutes from home) than it is at Newark, though an otherwise apparently aimless young man on the other side of the road was trying to pull weeds out from the gaps between the pavement slabs. Then I noticed that I'd chosen a place immediately outside one of those old Victorian mansions that was probably a very reputable hotel in times past but which maybe does not quite attract the same clientele these days. I wondered if I should have gone for the £4 per day car park, down an adjacent side street.

The reason I'd chosen Retford as my starting point was that it was only 15 minutes on the train to

Doncaster, and I was determined to make my way back in gently. I was hoping not to have to rub shoulders with anyone at all, actually, least of all with any blasé and asymptomatic youngsters just back from an anti-vaxxers' demo', or even a night club, come to think of it. To my relief, there was just one customer in front of me in the queue to buy a ticket. He was being attended to at the only booking office window that was open - or rather it was closed and visibly very well-sealed from the waiting area, but linked to the outside world by an audio system that gave a rather alien and metallic ring to his voice. Unfortunately, the guy two metres ahead of me was buying the shop, so by the time it was my turn people were steadily piling up behind me - but at a safe distance, I noticed, as I gingerly glanced over my shoulder. Like me, they were obediently all wearing masks, as requested.

My open return at £8.55 finally secured, I was on a platform and with a mission once again and it felt wonderful. Through the underpass to number two platform for northbound trains, where I was separated from the action on the up platform and the through lines by an ugly and apparently unnecessary white, diagonally slatted, six-foot fence that stretches the whole length of the platform. What on earth is that all about? It effectively cuts the station up into three curiously disjointed parts. A lengthy pathway from platform one leads down an incline to platforms three and four serving the Worksop to Lincoln line, which passes under the East Coast Main Line to the south of the main station building. When I first came to Retford, in 1963, there was a diamond crossing here, which the rail underpass replaced soon afterwards. What a hotchpotch the resulting station is, overall, in spite of the attractive and spacious façade and the wide southbound platform, set on quite a sharp curve.

Class 802 Number 802218, a 5-car bimodal belonging to Trans-Pennine Trains, was on crew training/route familiarisation and it soon moved off north in its cheery blue livery. Lurking behind it in the siding was one of the ubiquitous, yellow Network Rail machines that now do all the jobs that armies of permanent way men used to undertake in the past to help keep the railway safe.

There followed my first ride on an Azuma, which was on its way to York. I'd read about the supposedly uncomfortable straight-backed seats, but for a short time, anyway, mine seemed fine. I couldn't see any other passengers wearing a mask, though the attendant was and the bloke that went to the loo put one on to do so. The acceleration on the Azuma was notable and I liked the tinted windows that cut out the glare on this sunny morning, and the general cleanliness and subdued overhead lighting contributed to a favourable overall first impression.

We whizzed over Bawtry viaduct and past the children's playground where I'd spotted trains on the ECML in the spring of 1963, staying at the youth hostel that was just up the road. Before the light had faded that evening in early June, we had scrambled up to the edge of the ballast just in time to make out the name and number plate of A1 Class No. 60157 Great Eastern, her fire door open and shedding warm, red light throughout the cab and onto the surrounding smoke and steam. She crawled by us, just feet away, recovering from a signal check on her approach to the viaduct from the south. It provided another one of those moments that remain precious for ever.

In 2015, I had taken a day trip to Doncaster from Newark. It was the first time for fifty-two years that I had spent any length of time on the station, other than for changing trains whilst travelling through. Class A1 No. 60128 Bongrace had been one of the first engines we saw when we arrived on that day in 1963. If my memory serves me, she was drifting down towards the sheds alongside what was then the main London King's

Cross-bound platform and is now the bi-directional number three, passing an English Electric Type 4 sitting on the up fast centre road and a DMU at the opposite platform.

The presence of the Deltics and the English Electric Type 4s was the main reason that we only saw one Class A4, No. 60018 Sparrowhawk, when we bunked round the sheds later on in the day. We weren't keen on the EE4s. In our schoolboy logic, it was their fault that the Prinnies (Princess Royal Class) had already all gone, and the Semis (Coronation Pacifics), which had shared the crack expresses out of Liverpool Lime Street with them, would also soon be a thing of the past. Doncaster was every bit as busy on that day in 2015 as it had been in 1963. It was still attracting the spotters, too. I counted at least one for every year I had been away, almost all of them being around my age. Some had brought their fold-up camping chairs with them. I wondered if any of them were also present when I last sat on the platform here.

On the day, I had decided that Grand Central's black and orange was the most attractive and certainly the most stately express passenger livery on show, following the then relatively recent demise of the dignified navy blue of the former Great North Eastern Railway. Taken from roughly the same spot as the shot of Bongrace, overlooking the four-track main line between the two island platforms and with the overhead power lines being the most obvious addition to the scene over the intervening decades, a First Trans Pennine Class 185, No. 185117, was leaving the station in the direction of Sheffield.

What a lovely way to spend a few hours on a typical British summer's day, with bright sunlight, intermittent high clouds and a bit of a breeze. I found a seat at the south end of platform three, where I thought it would be relatively quiet and the footfall less. My tummy was rumbling already. In the spotting days of my youth, it was usually an early start and very difficult to make whatever provisions I had brought with me for the day last much past 11.00. The clock on the wall of the Plant, as Doncaster locomotive works is known, showed 11.40, so I resolved to wait until mid-day.

There still seemed to be a number of Class 91s around. Their demise is taking longer than I had thought was intended. Class 66s took freights north and south, No. 66150 swinging over the through lines as all the cross-country departures do, when going south west. Meanwhile, Class 67 No. 67028 sat in front of the Plant with chocks under one of her bogies, suggesting a problem with her braking system. No "chocks away" in her case, just yet then.

Suddenly, a kerfuffle ensued. A man had embarked on a King's Cross-bound Azuma just in front of me, hotly pursued by a ticket inspector. "That man does not have a ticket", he exclaimed to anyone within earshot. Both men then reappeared from the train, and another ticket collector, this one carrying a mobile ticket machine, engaged with the bloke who was in such a hurry to get to London. The transaction then took place on the platform, by which time the Azuma had left, and he had to wait for the next one. I glanced again at the Plant clock. It hadn't moved an inch but my phone confirmed that it was lunch time - a sandwich accompanied by a packet of crisps was the perfect combo, especially when taken at the platform end.

Doncaster station, now a Grade II listed building, was constructed by the Great Northern Railway and opened in 1849. Its present form dates from 1938, however, and it has since received a face lift that included a re-vamp of the concourse and the provision of a direct link to the Frenchgate shopping centre; changes that were officially recognised with a blue plaque, in 2007. Further changes were added in 2015 with the addition of platform 0, which arguably sounds almost as daft as platform nine and three quarters.

I was struck by how frequently trains to the capital were leaving, though not unexpectedly most did not stop at Retford. I was happy to bide my time and wait for a mid-afternoon return. Most of these services used platform one. My southbound Azuma was almost as full as main line trains used to be. I looked for masks but there very few and certainly not on the young man directly in front of me who was making a very animated business call for the benefit of the whole carriage. I adjusted my face covering and hoped he'd been double jabbed. Fifteen minutes is too long to hold your breath, unless you're an Indian Ocean pearl diver - reminding me of what fabulous names the Class A2s had and how many of them I never got to see before they were scrapped. I waited fairly uncomfortably for about 12 minutes and at the first hint of the train slowing for the Retford stop, I darted towards the relative safety of the vestibule, separated from the rest of the open carriage by sliding doors. Before I left, I noticed that the couple on the other side of the aisle from me had now both put their masks back on, while matey was still shouting into his phone.

Since this most recent visit, The Danum Gallery, Library and Museum in Doncaster has become host to a new Rail Heritage Centre to mark Doncaster's historical and strategic importance within the railway industry. Partnership with the National Railway Museum has provided the National Collection's Class V2 No. 60800 Green Arrow as the centrepiece of the display. This development was the outcome suggested by an earlier temporary exhibition we had visited in the Frenchgate Shopping Centre in the winter of 2017, when a significant part of the well-known Doncaster Grammar School Railway Collection, which itself now makes up an important part of the museum, was on view. The new centre was formally opened in September 2021.

Back in Retford, I retrieved my car, which I had almost every confidence would still be in one piece, and made for home. How nice was that, I mused, while mulling over my day out. I was back on track, at last, and I had felt that I really belonged, just like before.

3. Worksop

I'd been meaning to go back to Worksop for ages. I had worked there with autistic young adults for six years, between 2006 and 2011. One of the things we liked to do during that time was go to the station in the minibus, park up in one of the designated specs that was unofficially reserved for the buffet on platform two, put a scrap of paper on the dashboard explaining who we were and where we could be found, and then pile into the homely and very reasonably priced café for a spot of lunch.

The premises were decorated with framed photographs of steam trains taken at the station – both from the fifties and sixties and into the preservation era. There was a couple of shed plates from the local area on the walls, a few well-thumbed railway books on the window sill for anyone with time to browse and a three-dimensional wall plaque of an ancient passenger train on the Hull and Barnsley Railway above a window. An unofficial railway club met there on a Monday morning to talk about the old days, though they seemed relatively disinterested in what the traffic through the station was like in the present millennium. Every now and then, someone would venture outside to take a picture of a Class 66 diesel trundling through with a coal train. I got the feeling that as long as something was still moving through the station it was providing a useful tangible link with the past. As a train man, myself, all this suited me just fine.

For our learners, it was probably just one café out of many that they were comfortable to enter, and more importantly perhaps, one that we felt they could be sufficiently relaxed in for the amount of time necessary to order and eat lunch. Dealing with young people with autism was all about planning. They generally liked to take their time over things and we were used to preparing them for our next move with a series of announcements to that effect made beforehand. Nor was this just frivolous entertainment for those of us in charge. Access to the normal workings of the community was often quite a challenge for those with autism. Learning to cope with the unpredictability of social interactions when out and about was critical. Otherwise, the range of possible activities that they were able to enjoy became much more restricted. The only way to learn it was to reinforce it successfully, time after time.

It was now nearly five months since my first successful venture, back on track. The Covid business rattled on regardless in the meantime, with wave after wave of infection, both nationally and globally. Vaccinations in January and April 2021 and a booster jab in December had given us the confidence to travel around again rather more freely. Between May and the end of 2021, Chris and I had stayed in self-catering locations in Carmarthenshire, St Ives, Ironbridge and Coldstream and in hotels (briefly) at Ickworth near Bury-St-Edmunds and on Southport promenade. As before, we were really enjoying discovering and re-discovering Britain at our leisure. In each case during this time, though, we had been travelling by car.

Since my last trip, I had read that the scientists were having difficulty finding definitive instances of people becoming infected through touching surfaces where living

Coronavirus virus was just waiting to be picked up. It seems that there is something approaching unanimous agreement now that the overwhelming number of cases are direct person to person transmissions, which is what I suppose we have suspected all along. Nevertheless, I shall continue with the sanitising gel where it is made available and with a generally higher level of hand hygiene than before the pandemic. That must be viewed as a good thing in itself, and cut down on the spread of all sorts of other bacteria.

Just when things seemed to be heading in the right direction, however, the latest spanner in the works is now the Omicron variant. On the face of it, it appears to be more contagious again, but less virulent. The Government's online Coronavirus dashboard showed that on the day of my Worksop trip there were 189,213 new cases announced for the previous 24-hour period. More ominously, hospital admissions were starting to rise steadily once more. Though most of those infected have not been vaccinated, that is not the complete story, as many of those affected have already been inoculated, too. The government has stressed how important a booster jab is to try to keep on top of things.

The latest guidance is for face coverings to be worn on public transport, as before, a directive managed by about half those travelling from Nottingham to Worksop on 30th December 2021, when I joined the 15.21 from Whitwell, Derbyshire, for the 12-minute journey along the Robin Hood line. A few of those on board were wearing their masks round their chins and one or two with mouth covered but nose not, which seems to make little sense. I recently upgraded my masks, having read that simple cloth affairs give limited protection when compared with those of an FFP2/KN95 standard, and on the basis that each minor consideration could be the critical one in keeping safe.

There was plenty of room in the station car park and just one other passenger waiting for the train. I bought my ticket at a machine in the bus shelter affair on the platform, the first time I can remember ever doing this. The East Midlands Railway website urges paperless ticket purchasing rather than printing off your own booking at home prior to travelling, and one would presume they would also prefer to minimise any contact with the guard at the moment, as well, which may be why my travel status was not questioned by anyone in officialdom on the day.

The 3-car Class 170 unit arrived 6 minutes late. Warm, air-conditioned and comfortable, it was carrying very few passengers, which suited me fine. There was just one young man in my section of the carriage, unmasked and on his phone. I found a corner as far away from him as I could. The 170s are an improvement on the 2-car units used on this line previously, even though this example of cascading downwards from other routes as new stock is added to the overall fleet was looking rather tired and worn as far as its upholstery and fitments were concerned. At least, it looked and felt clean.

I had actually postponed this trip a number of times during the autumn. I'd been on the look-out on the admirable Realtime Trains website for a freight train through Worksop at a reasonable time of the day that I could go and photograph. To cut a long story short, where they were once plentiful, they are now few and far between. When visiting Worksop station over a decade ago, as well as frequent passenger trains to Nottingham, Sheffield and Lincoln, there was the regular rumble of Class 66 hauled coal, gypsum and other heavy goods and their returning empties. They really were quite a common sight, reminding me how much the energy market has changed again in such a short time. Megawatt Valley, the line of coal-fired power stations alongside the River Trent, is rapidly becoming a thing of the past, with only two left, at the time of this visit. West Burton is due to finish production in 2022, followed by Ratcliffe-on-Soar two years later.

One of the local colliery to power station routes through Worksop in times past started from Thoresby pit, which was at the end of a short spur connecting it to the former Lancashire, Derbyshire and East Coast Railway, east of Edwinstowe. From there, West Burton-bound merry-go-round wagons headed west to join the ex-Midland Railway at Shirebrook, turned north to Shireoaks East Junction and then east through the town and down into the Trent valley.

This had been made possible by the efforts of William Arkwright of Sutton Scarsdale Hall near Chesterfield. Towards the end of the nineteenth century, he had been looking for suitable rail links to take out the coal that lay beneath his country pile. Unable to come to a convenient arrangement with the existing railway companies, he had decided to go it alone. Edward Watkin of the Manchester, Sheffield and Lincolnshire Railway, who would no doubt have had his own axe to grind, called the bill setting up the LD&ECR "as mad a scheme as was ever presented to parliament". Arkwright's brain child did get off the ground but it never looked like matching up to its ambitious cross-country plans. It only existed as a separate entity for ten years before being taken over by the Great Central Railway in 1907.

The line west from Shirebrook to Chesterfield and the tracks east from High Marnham Power Station to Pyewipe Junction on the western edge of Lincoln, closed to passengers in stages during the 1950's, though summer weekend holiday traffic continued up until 1964. In 2014, UK Coal announced that Thoresby Colliery, up to that time the sole remaining deep level coal mine in Nottinghamshire, would close in July 2015, so I went along on 18th June to check it out while there was still time.

My Ordnance Survey map showed me the way down to the sidings and spur. I found the turning I needed on the A6075. It had a metalled surface but there was no indication of where it led to. Past the last house, the road became a track, but it was still drivable. Over a bridge that crossed a stream, through an open gate at the end and I had not passed any obvious place to park. I knew I had now just strayed onto railway property. The signalman's car was parked there with what looked like taxi markings, along with a white van labelled "Network Rail". There was just enough room for me. I went to talk to the driver of the van, who was reading a newspaper. I told him why I was there. I had looked on the internet and was expecting one coal train out and one train of empties in during the next half an hour. I asked if it would be OK to leave my car there for a few minutes while I took a couple of photos. He said he could not give me permission, but he didn't tell me to go, either. We chatted about his job, checking the workings of the mechanical signal boxes along the line. He was based at a location on the main line about ten miles to the east. His next port of call was the box directly to the west of this one, but he was in no hurry to get there. He gave me the impression that he did not get on too well with the signalman. Consequently, he intended to reduce his visiting time to that of a surgical strike.

Conversation turned to the advantages of the traditional signalman's life, which modern technology was in the middle of bringing to an end and which was the real reason I was there – to record it before it disappeared. It was a lovely summer's day. I had already heard skylarks and yellowhammers and seen tree sparrows in the few minutes I had been standing there. During my only other later visit there, but this time from the footpath behind Thoresby Colliery signalbox and so on the other side of the lines, an osprey flew right over my head. It was an (almost) idyllic rural oasis, yet only minutes from sizable settlements.

The NR man walked over the tracks to the signalbox for his chat with the signalman. I noticed that the locomotive, Class 66 No. 66613, having brought empty wagons into the sidings and then run round them on an adjacent track, was now moving slowly towards me to couple up with the other end of the rake, so I picked up the camera from my car. The signalman appeared at the door of his box and shouted at me. "Do you mind standing on the other side of your car, please, mate?" "OK", I replied, though a little puzzled, and I did what I was told. The engine rumbled forward. I took a couple of pictures but the light was wrong to begin with and my newly withdrawn position nearly scuppered the whole operation.

The NR man returned to his van. He explained that the driver might have reported me as a "near miss", and if he had, "We'd have had everyone here, swarming around the place". I murmured something generally compliant and wondered what they had me down as - demonstrator, suicide, terrorist, vandal or metal thief? NR man drove off to forge a meaningful, if short-lived and no doubt a little strained, working arrangement with his colleague in the next box. When the dust settled, I followed him back down the track to civilisation.

On my way home, I pondered over what the signalman in the next box might have said to upset NR man and wondered how that call was going. I also thought about how suspicious these two railwaymen had been of me. Surely, I don't look like a trouble maker? They were only covering their own backs, I concluded. They were doing their job by the book. I was strictly a trespasser on railway property. It is not just technology that has changed over the years. I'm all in favour of safer working practices, but we seem to have lost something of value along the way. Maybe, it is just trust.

It was not all bad news for the old LD&ECR, however. It was handed a lifeline east of Edwinstowe in 2009 in the form of the High Marnham Test Track, based at Lodge Lane, Tuxford. Network Rail now uses the 10.5-mile stretch from Thoresby Colliery Junction for testing engineering vehicles.

As we swung off the ex-Midland Railway's metals to join the former Great Central Railway route at Shireoaks South Junction in the approach to Worksop, the recent transformation of this area became apparent. What used to be rows of graffitied coal hoppers are now lines of withdrawn passenger stock. In amongst them was Class 47 No. 47715 in Network South East livery, which is retained for train heating purposes, or - more precisely - to keep carriage stock warm and aired. Chris and I once had a cab ride in a Class 47. It remains the only time I have ever had one in a diesel locomotive. It was at Newton Abbot in August 1979. We were staying at a guest house in Teignmouth and we had been on the train to Paignton for the day. On the way back, our train stopped at Newton Abbot and Chris asked me if we had to change for Teignmouth. I said no, mistakenly thinking that it was a through train, but we ended up instead in the sidings at Hackney Yard, where the stock was obviously (by then) being stabled. The Class 47 uncoupled from the train and started to run back past us along the adjacent track. I stuck my head out of the window to attract the driver's attention. He pulled to a halt alongside us and we transferred our eleven-month-old son, his buggy and ourselves into the cab. The driver then took us back to the platform at Newton Abbot. Though I felt a bit sheepish at my error, I was also quite pleased to get my one and only, totally unexpected diesel locomotive cab ride.

By the time our Class 170 had joined the line from Sheffield at Shireoaks East Junction, the impact that investment from the Harry Needle Railroad Company is having on Worksop was perfectly clear. Sidings on both sides of the line are packed with displaced rolling stock, stored stock, brand new stock and locomotives and stock being maintained and repaired. New buildings have been constructed and the place seems to be a hive of activity. Some deliveries of stock to HNRC also come in by road. Their website also makes it abundantly clear that this is a secure site and safe from unwelcome visitors (whatever their motives). I noticed Class 92 Nos. 92021/40/5/6 and Class 73 No. 73134 (at least some of which seemed to be minus their bogies) at the Worksop station end of the site and also a Pacer unit and a number of Class 08 shunters.

Sight of the withdrawn Pacer unit in the HNRC yard, no doubt now rescued for an afterlife elsewhere, reminded me of a trip we took on one some years ago, starting, in fact, from Worksop, itself. They are now being flung far and wide, as heritage railways pick up the otherwise redundant units as both spacious and cheap alternatives to previous generations of multiple units. Bouncy, bouncy was how I described our trip to Sheffield at the time, adding that they were soon to be pensioned off to be replaced by proper trains. I had always viewed them as too "bus-like" and therefore as curiosities, although I know they have always had their following. On that day, the heater wasn't heating, a draught whistled round the cavernous interior throughout the journey and the rain seemed to be falling on both sides of the window, even though the top vent was closed. We lurched and swayed over the points all the way to Sheffield.

Our EMR-liveried Class 170 crossed over to platform 2, where it had just two minutes left of its intended 6 minutes planned stopover time, before it was due to head out back to Nottingham, as the 15.39. I just had time to take a picture of No. 170419 while the drivers changed shifts, having witnessed them enjoying the briefest of chats half-way along the platform and outside our old cafe. There was no time for me to even peek my head round the door or take a photo of the station frontage, as intended, relying instead on a picture taken at another time.

The National Heritage Grade II listed Worksop station building was opened in 1849 by the Sheffield and Lincolnshire Junction Railway, itself part of the Manchester, Sheffield and Lincolnshire Railway, which in turn became the Great Central Railway in time for further extension, including more buildings that were added in 1900. The pedestrian bridge and the level crossing of Carlton Road at the platform end, as well as Worksop East signalbox, also Grade II listed, all help give the eastern end of the station its undoubted character.

The impressive station frontage to the rear of platform one is built of local stone which looks very similar to the magnesian limestone from the former nearby quarries at North Anston that was used for the building of the Houses of Parliament. With Dutch influenced gable ends as added decoration, it is of a rather splendid linear design, befitting its position at the heart of the Dukeries. Today, it fronts onto an extensive car park.

I took my seat in a deserted section of the front carriage. I sat and thought about all the time I'd spent here at Worksop station in the past, drinking coffee and coaxing our charges through another lunch time out in the community. My time in the town had been a massive eye opener for me. For the first time, I had worked closely with colleagues from very different backgrounds, people with a variety of skills that they brought from their previous occupations, including a couple of former coal miners.

They would wax lyrical and without prompting about the camaraderie that had been lost when the collieries closed. There were plenty of stories about mutual support and good neighbourliness and the way that the older miners dealt with youngsters entering the mines for the first time. The initiation ceremonies and the supposedly necessary toughening up process, as the older hands might have preferred to interpret the verbal bullying and gratuitous violence that was meted out to those coming in from school, made me wince. It was way outside my own experience.

Around the same time, I had been looking forward to enjoying a day out of school on a "jolly" - a fact-finding mission for teachers, although in truth, I was somewhat apprehensive about what lay ahead. I really did not find it much fun underground at Bentinck Colliery in 1983. After a lengthy underground train journey, we had to walk, rather stooped, for the rest of the way to the coal face. It was dark, dusty and hot. Once there, we had to get down on our knees and crawl one after the other along the line of the face, beneath and between the aluminium cantilevered pit props that held up the roof and through an area where the coal had only recently been removed. It seemed to go on for ages. It was uncomfortable, claustrophobic and there was now absolutely nowhere you could stand up, which I found very disconcerting. We passed the coal-cutter in action and the men carried on with their tasks as though we were not there. The miners seemed to be spread out along the face and the belt that served it, rather than clustered round the working machinery itself. The lights attached to the head-gear darted around in the gloom, and water was being sprayed around and dripping off the roof, presumably to dampen down the dust. As we moved on to the end of the seam that was being worked, the roof itself repeatedly creaked and groaned. It sounded like it was going to collapse at any minute, but it satisfied itself with periodically dropping an odd fragment of rock or suddenly choosing to pile up a hillock of smaller dusty debris in a short-lived but steady trickle from the roof. I was glad to get out. The thought of working long shifts day after day in that environment was actually quite distressing. I would have hated it and I was glad I would never have to do it.

We got showered and changed and were taken for a free lunch at British Coal's Eastwood Hall headquarters and then to an afternoon board-room session with National Union of Mineworkers man, Roy Link, who was obviously someone approved by the company for that purpose. I was to see a lot more of him on television in the years that followed, as the union itself fractured in Nottinghamshire, as part of an acrimonious battle between working and striking miners.

I had my moments in school during this troubled time, as well, for example, when teaching the energy question to an "A" level class that included the daughter of a working miner and the girlfriend of one who was on strike. We were certainly discussing people's livelihoods in a way that mattered. My subject came to life like never before. The strike called by the leaders of the NUM in response to supposed government intentions for wholesale pit closures lasted a year. The government declared the strike illegal and withdrew benefits from striking miners. Many families went through real hardship during that time. The schism in Nottinghamshire that led to the setting up of the Union of Democratic Mineworkers just made matters worse, in terms of the prevailing atmosphere in the pit communities.

A mass rally was called by the NUM, and the strikers - many of whom stayed out for a whole year - and their supporters marched through Mansfield, where I was working at the time. Windows were apparently put in when they marched past some of the downtown pubs that were suspected as being the meeting places for UDM members. I wandered down after school. Everyone had gone, but the area had become a wasteland. There was litter strewn everywhere, including food wrappers, cans, bottles, posters, hand-outs and the remains of placards. It was all over the closed roads as well as the pavements. I was told that fans from certain other clubs coming to play at Nottingham Forest still chanted "scabs" at the locals. It is extraordinary how deeply that division was felt and how it has still not been forgotten, or obviously even forgiven, in certain circles.

Twenty-five years later, when I was walking down Worksop's streets with some regularity, in the company of our youngsters from college, I wrote down my own impressions of the place. "This is a dump. On a cold, damp, grey day it is even worse. Too many closed shop units, even the post office has closed - mind you it did smell of wee. How can that be? There are some visibly very poor and angry people scowling at me. A disconsolate cluster is hanging around the foot of a flight of steps that leads up to the employment agency. The pavement around them is littered with pigeon shit, fag ends and chewing gum. There is a sign in the greengrocer's shop window, "Missing – dog with three legs". Lairy youths swear and shout insults across the road at each other. In the pedestrianised town centre, which is really the paved main street, is a seat with a dedication to Nelson Mandela. He must be the super hero with the most dedications in the world, from schools to roads to this final accolade, a seat in Worksop, but what would he have thought of it here? Worksop's pedestrian area has more cars on it than anywhere else I've seen so described. This is because blue badge holders can ignore the restriction and there are loads of them, yet, perplexingly, the council will not provide our college for youngsters with autism with one for our minibus. There is now a traffic jam in the pedestrianised zone! That is a contradiction in terms. Now they are beeping at each other. I overhear a conversation which starts, 'Let's see your tattoo?' 'It's itching like fuck'. I've also just spotted an elderly couple with his and hers mobility scooters, so that's a first. Take extra care driving through here. People walk out into the road oblivious of you and by no means all drivers bother with their indicators at all. In Iceland, the woman I am stuck behind in the check-out queue absolutely reeks. On a previous visit, I saw a blind man with a stick wearing an i-pod with headphones. Perhaps that's good policy in Worksop. Remove your senses from the reality of it all as completely as you can". I ended my observations by writing "Beam me up, Scotty".

One of the ex-miners on our staff was always after a laugh, though his amusement could often be at my expense - or anyone else's who was on hand. On one occasion, we stopped with our van full of learners at a well-known confectioners. I was asked to stay in the van while he bought the sandwiches for lunch. He went in and told the lady who was serving that I had complained vehemently about the quality of the last sandwich I had bought from there and had vowed never to go there again. He wound the assistant up about it so much that she stormed out of the shop, approached my side window and gave me a tirade about my complete lack of respect for her products. My companion got back in, drove off and laughed his way to our destination at the effectiveness of the trap he had set.

At such times, he would also reminisce fondly about the time when the pits were all working, though he also reminded us that it had always been a dangerous occupation. A workmate had died in a pit roof fall. He was 24 years old, had three children and had just invested in a little shop. "There were some fit blokes there who cycled to work, shifted 20 tons of coal, cycled home and then went to play sport or work on their allotments. They seemed to see through their whole working lives, as well". He had enjoyed taking footplate rides with the "auld fellas" who drove the colliery tank engines around the sidings, shunting the coal wagons. He recalled about how much they valued their jobs at the pit head, rather than being underground. Many of them were also railway enthusiasts, some of whom had gone on to be serious railway modellers in their spare time. Unfortunately, they would soon have much more spare time than they had envisaged.

Our caretaker was also an ex-collier. He told me about an accident at one of the 10 pits in which he had worked. A cage carrying about 32 men plummeted to the bottom of the shaft when the brakes failed, "killing about half 'n 'em". He had missed entering the cage by one person, because he had been chatting to another miner about whippets. At another pit he had worked at, he avoided, by one shift, becoming involved in a roof collapse which killed five men. He knew he had been lucky.

The urban landscape in Worksop has visibly changed

since those days, with a modern library, bus station and cinema, and all with pleasing modern designs, full of flashing, sun-filled reflections from acres of glass. I'm not close enough to judge if the town has fully recovered from the traumas imposed on it a generation ago. Whether your blame for the travails inflicted on it was directed at Thatcher or Scargill, the result was undoubtedly severe hardship for the former coalfield communities, which lasted for decades.

I had thought it wise to avoid the rush hour for the short journey back to Whitwell. Leaving Worksop behind me once more, I settled back into my seat and enjoyed 9 minutes of solitude, staring out into the early dusk of a dismally dark and drizzly December day. I was back on track again and I'd just got one in, as I'd hoped to, before the end of the year. What can we look forward to in 2022, I wondered? Who could have predicted, just two years before, how everyday life would have changed in the way that it has?

One sunny afternoon later on in January 2022, I returned to Worksop by road. I had been assured online that a locomotive-hauled train was on its way. Class 56 No. 56081 duly pulled up on time alongside platform 2 with a new Class 720 Aventra electric multiple unit No. 720544, fresh from a running-in session on the Old Dolby test track and marked up for Greater Anglia. All things come to those who wait - eventually.

Back home once again, I reflected on the damning verdict I had imposed on downtown Worksop, although it was already many years ago, now. I know that it appeared rude, harsh and dismissive. In fact, I had felt exasperated that the situation I described had been allowed to happen at all. People had been badly let down and their justifiable resentment was very evident. They came over as defeated and dejected. Poverty was rife and the impression I got was that many of the inhabitants had simply given up.

Anywhere else that had experienced such rapid de-industrialisation must have suffered from similar levels of deprivation and with a range of social problems as a result. My despairing observations would undoubtedly have been mirrored elsewhere, and so it felt somehow unfair to be picking on Worksop, specifically. Nevertheless, it was a personal snapshot of how one rather unlovely and unloved place had struck me at that particular moment in time. It provided me with the antithesis of my own personal notion of a love of place. It was also important to realise that it was part of a much bigger story. You could not have made it up - and I hadn't.

4. Newark

The mid-morning temperature had surged from minus one to zero degrees Celsius by the time I left the house for Fiskerton station. Bright sunlight had given way to mist by Southwell and it was decidedly foggy another three miles further on into the Trent valley. When I had tried this trip on a sunny day earlier in the week, I had discovered that the road was closed off at both ends of the station car park while Severn Trent Water dug a big hole, so I had gone back home. What else could possibly go wrong this time? I found out later that the coal train from Immingham docks that I'd hoped to photograph was two hours late leaving the port, explaining its no-show at lunchtime in Newark.

All was not lost, however. The Class 156 two-car unit No. 158852 from Stoke – it should have been from Crewe but the first section had been cancelled – arrived on time at Fiskerton station at 12.22. Before embarking, I'd just had enough time to look over the wonky signalbox again, still in situ with frame and levers intact, but without its interior signalbox diagram or the external signalbox board that disappeared very soon after it became defunct, following re-signalling and the installation of automatic level crossing barriers in the summer of 2018. This is how I described it on a very different sort of a day, weatherwise….

Well, will you look at it? Was there ever anything like it anywhere else in the country? This is (or, rather, was) Fiskerton level crossing gate keeper's signalbox in

Nottinghamshire on the old Midland Railway route from Nottingham to Lincoln, known nowadays as the Castle Line. The box was constructed in 1902. The crossing and the accompanying semaphore signals were, until a year or so ago, manually operated by the signalman. Now out of commission, it won't be there for much longer because progress will have swept it all away - unless it is swallowed up from below in the meantime.

The lamp standard and the old concrete level crossing gate post add a vertical dimension to this skew-whiff centrepiece. It was a hot day when I took the photograph. The signalman was entertaining a Network Rail colleague and the signalbox door was wide open. I wondered if they might be suffering from a bit of sea sickness or vertigo in there. If too many people stand towards the rear, is the box in danger of capsizing? Could you perhaps fall backwards rather too easily when pulling the levers?

I had actually called by a few months earlier and had a chat with the signalman about Network Rail's up-grading plans. He had kindly invited me inside. He was only too well aware of the heritage which surrounded him and which was soon to be lost. There were photographs of steam specials passing the location, given to him by enthusiasts and pinned up on the wall. He was proud to show me round. I vowed to return with my camera to record the features on the inside of the box while it was still working and he welcomed the idea.

Unfortunately, on the next two occasions that I went down there, different employees were on duty and no such invitation was forthcoming. In fact, the largely mono-syllabic responses I received to my friendly opening lines put me off even asking. Whilst trying to avoid becoming known as the local signalman stalker, I did eventually find a friendly face and duly took some photos.

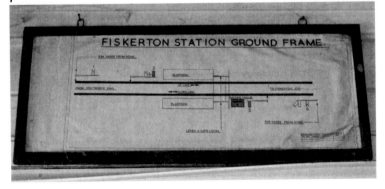

The signalbox diagram was in a style common to the interiors of all boxes, of course, and Fiskerton's ground frame layout was placed above the levers, as was the usual practice.

Soon after I had taken my pictures, Network Rail took possession of the crossing, the road was closed and the old procedures for opening and closing the gates quickly became a thing of the past, as is happening across the country. The mechanical systems were then replaced with automatic barriers and colour light signals. The inside of the box had looked quite homely, assisted by the provision of some net curtains – perhaps a nice piece of quality Nottingham lace, or possibly just someone's old tablecloth.

Previously, the signalman still had plenty to do, typical of many such locations. He had to brave the elements twice on each occasion that a train was due to pass through. The main gates were drawn across the road by hand and the smaller gates for pedestrians leading to the walkway over the crossing were also locked. Another pedestrian gate, a more recent addition, gave direct access to the up platform from the walkway. The signalman then returned to his cabin, signals were cleared and after the train had passed, all the procedures were reversed. Safety notices in the car park, which is on the down, Newark and Lincoln-bound side of the line, reminded intending passengers to leave sufficient time before their train was due to depart, because once the gates were closed for an approaching train, they would not be able to access the up platform.

Pictures on the internet show Fiskerton box in its pre-wonky period and indicating no signs of any inclination to sink into the ground. Quite when and why it decided on a less than vertical disposition is not clear. Network Rail, or their predecessors, Railtrack and before them British Rail, must have taken action at some stage to keep it the right way up. Two steel girders were driven through its sides beneath floor level and placed on the sections of old wooden sleepers that were piled up beneath the protruding ends. Clearly, it was a victory for the functional over the aesthetic. The resulting state of affairs might not have been quite the solution they were looking for, however, as the degree of tilting was certainly never rectified - not that it really matters any more.

Fast forward to 2022 and the box still stands at its jaunty angle next to the road crossing, as my train to Newark approached. I bought my ticket from the guard for the 12-minute journey to Newark Castle. There was a sprinkling of passengers on board, who were reassuringly all masked up, as the sign on the platform had insisted, pointing out that it is presently a legal requirement for all those travelling. There were 99,652 new cases of Coronavirus recorded on the 14th January 2022. This number has dropped quite rapidly over the last week after increasing just as quickly during the week before that. 2,423 people were admitted to hospital with Covid in the previous 24-hour period, bringing the total to 19,539 inpatients. This is more than twice the rate at the end of 2021. A further 270 deaths were recorded and this week's totals have been noticeably higher than previously, as well. It seems that the current wave is still strong, but at least showing signs of levelling off. I'm not inclined to take any unnecessary risks until things have subsided substantially once more.

Newark Castle station is a Grade II listed building
dating from 1846, the former Midland Railway's
Nottingham to Lincoln line having celebrated its 175th
anniversary in 2021. Constructed in the Italianate style,
it has been carefully restored, both inside and out. The
booking office now occupies the southern end, but most
of the available interior space is a comfortable café
called Carriages. When we had a snoop around in May
2018, the interior décor included the café's own in-
house designed coat of arms, in true railway company
heraldic tradition and set above the twin, central
fireplaces. This fine old building with its preserved,
cobbled street station approach, is a credit to all those
who ensured it was included in the redevelopment of
the riverside area of the town. Apart from the cars, the
scene looked positively Dickensian on the day, under
this pea-souper.

The main station in Newark, of course is not Castle but Northgate, even though the Midland Railway reached Newark first. The Great Northern Railway got there in 1850, traversing the MR Lincoln line on the flat crossing that still exists (as a bit of a nuisance to the railway operators, no doubt), just to the north of the town. Northgate's position on the East Coast Main Line has meant that I have made frequent visits there over the years. In 2013, I watched the LNER Class A4 Pacific No. 4464 Bittern pass through Newark Northgate at 92 m.p.h. I did not take a photo because I just wanted to wallow in the spectacle, uninterrupted. I have also caught up with a few other steam specials from time to time, including Britannia Class No. 70013 Oliver Cromwell on 22nd June 2013, Coronation Class No. 46233 Duchess of Sutherland in December 2016 and Royal Scot Class No. 46100 Royal Scot in April 2017.

I had even dropped in during June 2021 to see the new Azumas. "Here tomorrow", announced the email that LNER had sent me to promote the launch of the new service. I went along to Newark the next day to see them in action, as instructed, and to collect my Lucky Bag, as the message had also promised. "Starts tomorrow", said the eager young man on the station. There was nobody giving out freebies, either, but by chance, Class 800 No. 800112 was loitering on staff training or route familiarisation, so I got my photo.

When I had finally caught up with Royal Scot here, I was really quite excited about it. She was in the loop, waiting for her path southwards back to Southall, following a visit to the North York Moors Railway. I had never seen her before because she spent her last active BR days based on former Midland lines at Nottingham, when we were doing most of our spotting on the West Coast Main Line at Crewe and Preston. Now I only need to see 4 Scots out of the total of 71 class members, which, of course, is not going to happen.

There was quite a crowd on the station, as is often the case on such occasions. The station staff at Newark have generally been very helpful and welcoming in permitting access to the platforms for the viewing of steam specials, even when there were barriers. It is obviously good PR for the industry, reflecting the continued, widely held affection for our railway heritage amongst the public at large. I noticed a number of commuters who were clearly surprised by her presence but who had also bothered to stop to take their own photographs of her on their phones, presumably to share with friends and family. Rail fans often bring children and grandchildren to such events, nurturing an interest that will surely help to maintain the railway preservation movement in the future.

I haven't always gone onto the station itself to watch steam specials pass through Newark. Some years ago, I waited in the company of about twenty other people on the Sleaford Road bridge, south of the town centre, to celebrate a northbound run of the new-build Class A1 No. 60163 Tornado. The guy with the fancy video recorder mounted on a tripod, who had been training his sights for the previous half an hour on the curve in the Grantham direction around which she would finally appear, suddenly realised at the last minute that three people and a dog were now walking into his view finder and more particularly into ear-shot along the line-side footpath, and just below his strategically chosen position. "Excuse me, can you be quiet, please?" he demanded. The thing was that no-one was actually talking, or even barking. The only sound - apart from Tornado, which had just announced its imminent arrival with steam now visible above the trees and a just audible whistle - was the tapping on the ground of the disabled old lady's aluminium walking stick, securely strapped on at the elbow. She stopped abruptly, looked at her companions in disgust, lifted her stick into the air, stared at it pointedly and then glared back towards the source of the request in disbelief at what she had just heard. Perhaps that was one potential convert lost to the cause, I thought, as No. 60163 steamed resplendently under our bridge and disappeared in the direction of York. I'm pleased to report that the lady in question managed to remain firmly upright throughout the event. I doubt if she bothered to turn up for the return working that evening, though.

In February 2016, I had been at the same location for the return to steam after a lengthy and expensive overhaul of A3 Class No. 60103 Flying Scotsman, surely the world's most famous locomotive, with the possible exception of the Rocket. Again, and as I would do later with Bittern, I chose not to take photos but just immerse myself in the moment, untrammelled by gadgetry – just me and the locomotive. OK, well not just me, as it turned out, but you get the gist. Anyway, I've got loads of photos of her in other places and at other times.

My road journey to Newark always takes me past the pub in the next village with the chalk board outside, which, for as long as I can remember, has flagged up their "Fresh Whitby Cod", in spite of the fact that we couldn't possibly be any further from the sea. I visualise a regular special consignment - an express fish van with a police escort and flashing lights. Perhaps they temporarily close some roads, so as not to slow it down on its dash from North Sea to table in rural Nottinghamshire. Last week the notice was scrubbed out and replaced with an updated sales pitch, "New Menu Whitby Cod", so hopefully no less fresh.

Sleaford Road bridge is the most convenient ECML viewpoint I can reach from home and I have been here many times over recent years to witness the passing of steam hauled trains on this old racing ground.

Today's return of the Flying Scotsman is extra special. The A3s felt completely at home here from the 20s through to the 60s and though I was over the hills and far away at the time (for the 50s and 60s bit, anyway), I got across to see some of them, including this one, before they had almost all disappeared. For 50 years now, she has been the sole remaining member of her class and after her well documented recent problems she is with us once again. Virtually rebuilt, she is still essentially the Flying Scotsman, the railwaymen's own definition being the permanence of her frames.

Radio 5 Live has just broadcast a warning to onlookers not to trespass on the railway because its already leading to delays elsewhere on the network. There is more traffic than usual at the bottleneck roundabout on the A46 at the entrance to Newark and I quickly park up with 15 minutes to spare. There are literally hundreds of people here rather than the usual 20 or 30. The word is that she is late - 15 minutes, then 22 minutes. A class of kids from a junior school turns up, filing in two abreast behind their teacher. They just keep coming. It must be a whole school-full. The really naughty ones have to wear high-vis' jackets. I climb onto a roadside metal barrier so I can see over all the heads and I get a good view of the road, as well. Some motorists are clearly bemused, others smile, one or two beep their support. Only a few ignore the crowd completely. Orange-clad construction workers in hard hats have perched themselves on upper sections of their JCBs, which they have moved right up to the railings within the nearby work site. Three young blades in an old banger with the window wide open yell insults at the throng and then are immediately held up at the traffic lights. They may now be reconsidering their choice of expletives, though luckily for them they are simply ignored.

Northbound, a Class 91 passes at 10.40, followed by another at 10.43 and a third at 10.50, held up no doubt by the over-enthusiastic spectators mentioned on the radio bulletin. Some of the children cheer the Class 91 and I wonder if they have been properly briefed. At 10.59 a 5-car unit for Hull goes through and then, at last, at 11.04, the Scotsman appears. Her headlight is a powerful beam, even on a very bright day. White steam and smoke stand out against the blue and cloudless sky. The sunlight gleams off her newly painted boiler. A ripple of applause is answered by a thin and reedy whistle from the A3 (never their strong point). There are waves from the passengers and then she is gone. The helicopter and the three light aircraft that have been buzzing around disperse, as do the crowds. Amidst the smiles, the excited chatter and the checking of images on cameras, the crocodile of schoolchildren resumes its shape, as, at 11.09, a passing HST indicates that the railway is straight away back to normal.

I make my way back home. The Scotsman has returned to the NRM at York and Whitby cod is still on the menu. Some things may change, but the affection the people of this country have for their railways shows every sign of continuing. It is an engrained part of our history and culture. It helps to define who we are.

A year later, we were entertained at our local railway club by an octogenarian and former locomotive fireman, who first signed on with the LNER in 1947. In the 1950s, he often fired the Flying Scotsman during her stint on the Great Central lines, between Leicester Central and London Marylebone. She was shedded at Leicester Central, at the time. However, Flying Scotsman was not at the top of his list of favourite engines, nor those of the drivers he worked with. I've heard this a number of times over the years, that different steam engines from the same class often seemed to have very different personalities, revolving around their steaming attributes, their responsiveness to the controls and other idiosyncrasies that might not have been expected from a supposedly uniform design. He was adamant that Flying Scotsman had not been a "good 'un" and who am I to argue with that. She still looks good, though, even if the crew are having to work that little bit harder. She is certainly worth the effort.

In March 2018, I noticed that one of Northgate's best-known features, the old Potts clock on platform one did not know what time of day it was. In fact, it showed a different time on its two faces but both of them were wrong.

William Potts set up his clock making business in Leeds in 1833. The clocks were sold to cathedrals, town halls, schools and engineering works, as well as to the railways, both at home and abroad. As an iconic part of the platform one landscape at Newark Northgate for many a year, it must have seen every named Eastern Region locomotive under the sun stream by during the 50s and 60s, so there's a thought. Luckily, for the benefit of today's travellers there is an alternative digital affair to the Potts clock nearby, which appeared to be more closely related to GMT.

Northgate station was also our departure point for a particularly entertaining visit to the capital and this is how it unfolded. Quiet Coach B lived up to its name for the 12 minutes it was timetabled to travel from Newark to Grantham. The racket started as soon as the doors were opened. "This one, then. There are seats there". They stumbled aboard with rucksacks and bulging carrier bags, but no suitcases. "They're no good. They're all reserved. We'll have to split up". "Excuse me, this is the Quiet Coach", someone already comfortably seated bravely piped up. Reducing the pitch of their voices by about one decibel per person, they started to fan out down the carriage. "Some up here", claimed the pioneer, walking the full length of the coach towards our carefully chosen, reserved and labelled, window and aisle seats, facing the direction of travel.

"Are these taken?" she asked, staring first at the empty reservation card holders above the two seats opposite, then at us, before returning her glance to the seat backs in apparent disbelief that they really were vacant. "Look, six together. You go there", she motioned to the rest of her party. "We'll sit here…. Do you mind?", she implored, turning to lean over us, her bag already half on what I had already begun to regard as "our" table. A little reluctantly, I shuffled together the various sections of the Saturday newspaper. It felt like she was apologising in advance for the fact that it was no longer going to qualify for the description of Quiet Coach B. "I'm desperate for a coffee", her partner exclaimed, so drained by the process of finding six seats within shouting distance of each other that caffeine requirement levels had been raised to critical. "Mine's white with one sugar", came the sarcastic interjection from the other end of the Coach Formerly Known as Quiet Coach B.

All seated at last, out came the bottles of Buck's Fizz. The first cork to be removed ricocheted off the light fitments above our heads and shot off down the coach in the general direction of the most recent contributor to the conversation. It was accompanied from our end of the carriage by the sort of muffled laughter that naughty children employ when they have just been found out.

Thus began one of the rowdiest trips to London that Quiet Coach B had probably witnessed in quite a time. The subsequent entertainment was provided by a group of middle-aged party-goers, determined to start their day out in the metropolis in a manner that they clearly had every intention of maintaining throughout. From a range of containers, a vast picnic was assembled. "Would you like a cold sausage sandwich - these ones are veggie?" "No thanks, "I replied, "It's a bit too early in the day for me".

Of course, the quiet coach is a comparatively modern phenomenon and a response to the inconvenience caused to other customers by the proliferation of hand-held devices and the other apparently essential trappings of our technological age. In the past, the only way to escape the excessive noise levels associated with other members of the public, and especially the multitudes of excitable children being taken on holiday, was to be in possession of a first-class travel ticket. There was always something intriguing about those wide-open spaces and their spotless antimacassars, but my parents would certainly have never been able to afford to rest their heads against them when I was young.

Well in advance of our annual family holiday to the Lake District or Somerset, my dad bought our rail journey tickets at Frames, an agent for British Railways, which was opposite the famous NEMS record shop in Whitechapel in Liverpool, where the Beatles signed up with Brian Epstein in 1962, in the office belonging to the family business. Next door to Frames was the rambling Philip Son and Nephew book store, with its narrow and tortuous staircases. Though we may have been assured of a seat on the train, we were certainly not guaranteed peace and quiet. Every other seat in the carriage was likely to have been occupied and many holiday makers had to stand in the corridors or sit on their suitcases in the vestibules next to the loo at the end of the coach. With no air conditioning, it could get very hot and sticky on "Saturdays Only" trains in July and August, especially in the compartment stock, where heavily laden passengers tried to pass each other down already partially blocked corridors. Once settled, you could open the window if you gained the approval of those around you, but then there was the risk of more noise from the locomotive, a draught for those sitting downstream of it, as well as smoke and smuts on previously clean clothing. Add to that, the constant clickety-click, clickety-clack from the sixty-foot lengths, the repetitive metallic clunk as the wheel tappers got to work when we stopped at Preston or Shrewsbury, crackly public address announcements, engine and platform whistles and all that blowing off prior to departure. Gloriously eventful it was for me. Quiet, it was not.

Back in Quiet Coach B, the initial excitement had subsided and we chatted our way to the capital, though perhaps with some of us feeling a little more sheepish than others about talking at what might be described as normal volume. It transpired that our new friends did have reserved seats in coach B, had not realised it was nominally a quiet coach and had then found out that some of their seats were already occupied once they had embarked.

On our return journey from London the next day, the attendant broke off from wheeling the snacks trolley down the train to reprimand a young man who had infringed the rules of Quiet Coach B by taking a call on his mobile phone whilst still at his seat. "The ticket collector will have a word with you, so I'm just warning you", she offered, as non-confrontationally as she could manage.

So, what actually are the rules in Quiet Coach B? The website says "We have quiet coaches on all our trains for passengers who choose a more peaceful journey. These coaches provide a calm environment on board where you can work, relax or doze in peace. We request that people in the Quiet Coach are considerate to their fellow passengers by: keeping noise to a minimum, putting mobile phones on silent or vibrate, taking phone calls in the vestibule, using headphones to listen to music or watch videos, with the volume on low, and (finally, it says) talking quietly".

It is difficult to take issue with any of that, except to say that surely wherever you are on the train you should be considerate to other passengers and not just in QCB? Maybe I actually plumped for QCB with the expectation that it might be a little less noisy, but more likely, I think, hoping that it might be a little less crowded. It certainly did not feel like a particularly critical decision at the time that we booked it.

Strangely enough, the Quiet Coach B episode was probably not the most bizarre thing that I've witnessed on a journey beginning at Newark. Chris and I were in such good time for the London train, on which we had seats booked, that we were already waiting on the platform when the preceding King's Cross-bound express pulled in. A man in shirt sleeves carrying two cups of coffee (presumably) got off the train directly in front of us and headed straight for the coffee bar, a little further down the platform to our left. He returned, similarly laden, two minutes later, just as the doors were closing. As he moved forward towards the now closed doors, the station staff attendant who had already blown his whistle, shouted to him to stand back. "You can't just get on and off when you want", he added. "Do you think I care?", replied the man, suddenly the centre of attention but eager not to lose face in front of the by now bemused and amused onlookers. He then took a smart exit to the right and disappeared up the footbridge steps that lead from the island platform to the down side of the station and the entrance. Somewhere in coach E, his companion must have been wondering what had happened to his or her drink as they continued their journey to London alone - but presumably in the company of his jacket and any other of his now discarded belongings. We did not see the man reappear by the time our own train was ready to leave, a few minutes later. That was in December 2018 and it was not a warm day. Perhaps the first thing he did, having found himself marooned unexpectedly in Newark, was to drink two cups of coffee and then go and buy himself a coat.

Nothing remotely as dramatic happened on my scheduled 6-minute return trip from Newark Castle to Fiskerton in January 2022. All I could see through the gloom outside were posts for fencing, telephone and electricity cables, lineside trees and the beginnings of fields quickly disappearing into the fog. The guard on the 12.43 remembered me from the outward journey. He didn't even ask to see my senior railcard again. I could have been anyone under this lot, I thought, from behind my mask, steamed-up glasses, coat collar turned up and woolly hat pulled down, but my disguise hadn't fooled him for a second.

5. Nottingham

"Ladies and gentlemen, we are arriving in St Pancras five minutes early. We apologise if this causes any inconvenience. If you like, you can sit on the train for a while". I just loved that welcome to the capital, on one of a series of Midland Main Line trips we have made from Nottingham to London over the years.

Things have not always gone quite to plan on that route, however. In the days before Mansfield's own station was reinstated, I was leading a party of GCSE-aged schoolchildren from Alfreton and Mansfield Parkway for an overnight in Boulogne. Having clearly briefed them - or so I thought - about what was required when we arrived at Nottingham station, we all speedily disembarked from the feeder unit, hurried over the footbridge and boarded the connecting service just before the doors on the express train closed. The train promptly pulled out, passing two of our girls anchored to the platform. They were transfixed, just staring at their friends and teachers through the window, open-mouthed and jaws dropping, as the rest of the party were whisked out of sight. Negotiations with train staff and through them with station employees at Loughborough eventually allowed us to scoop the abandoned girls up off the following service, when it, too, reached St Pancras. That one still appeared in my dreams for sometimes afterwards, when I was awoken by the same sort of jolt to the senses that I felt on the day.

I drove down to Lowdham station after breakfast on a bright but cool January day. Recently added information panels informed me that Lowdham Railway Heritage have rescued the old 1896 Midland Railway signalbox from its former site on the Nottingham-bound side of the level crossing and repositioned it next to the station building on the other side of the line, where it is now open as a museum, on certain days.

The Midland Railway's Nottingham to Lincoln line was engineered by George Stephenson and opened in 1846. Lowdham station is a Grade II listed building which passed into private ownership in 1990. Many original features remain and some have been restored since then. The old station house has plenty of reminders of the Midland Railway, including a lamp standard, a boundary marker and a wall-mounted lantern with glass tablet, complete with an electric light bulb, so presumably it is still providing a useful function.

The wooden, MR poster board, complete with header, must be about 100 years old, though it looks as though it might have had some attention more recently. It appears to be double crown size (20 x 30 inches) rather than the more usual standard sized double royal, at 25 x 40. As a means of communicating information to the travelling public, it provides a stark contrast to the modern Help Point post that has recently been erected on the platform and is powered by sunlight. Partially hidden behind modern fencing, the running-in board - announcing to passengers that they have arrived at Lowdham - has not been refurbished. Its frame has gradually decayed and dropped off, it would seem, but the British Railways (Eastern Region) dark blue background is still visible, though much faded. It, too, has been superseded by the modern version of station signage alongside it.

These historic reminders of the age of steam on Lowdham station were the setting some years ago when I had wandered down in the car to watch a steam-hauled special returning from Lincoln to Tyseley. There can sometimes be a perceptible sideways movement of a steam locomotive at speed as it approaches you head on, which is as impressive as it can be slightly unsettling. Ex-GWR Castle Class No. 5029 Nunney Castle was going very well through Lowdham, but with as pronounced a rocking of this kind that I can ever remember seeing. I crossed my fingers that they had checked their clearances accurately, though it was an exciting sight, nevertheless.

It is never too late to inspire or be inspired by a steam train on the move. Round about the time of my Nunney Castle experience, I had noticed a clash on the calendar. My wife had arranged a get-together over coffee with our daughter's in-laws. Ex-GWR Hall Class No. 4965 Rood Ashton Hall was due to make one of its forays to Lincoln for the Christmas market. I was forced to run an alternative location for elevenses past the somewhat bemused couple that we were just getting to know. The new venue was now within walking distance of Bleasby station on the same ex-Midland Railway line from Nottingham to Lincoln, via Newark Castle. Coffee, teacakes and chat were duly undertaken, while I kept an eye on the clock. The day was bright and cold and we had purposely chosen the table next to the wood-burning stove.

A bit of a dilemma arose. If the special was early, as they sometimes can be, we were stumped, but I couldn't drag our new friends out onto the platform prematurely to risk their catching a cold for Christmas. We assembled with five minutes to spare, as always it seems on such occasions, to be joined by a knot of other steam fans, with three generations represented. There appears to be an unwavering assumption that small children will enjoy the sight and sound of a steam locomotive as much as their parents and grandparents do, which I find quite gratifying.

The Hall announced its presence from afar. There is a long straight section bearing down on Bleasby from Thurgarton. The nature of the day meant that the plume of smoke and steam was visible well before we could hear or see the locomotive herself. I turned and noticed that the automatic barriers were still open to road traffic and that there was no sound yet from the warning siren for approaching motorists. "I hope they're going to shut the gates, soon", I thought, out loud, not that "gates" were the best way to describe them. Number 4965 bore down on the functional, narrow and staggered concrete platforms at Bleasby as the warning sounded and the barriers fell, and I was able to relax and enjoy the scene at last.

Shiny Brunswick green paint and copper trimmings shone in the sunlight. Steam, smoke and the smell of hot oil momentarily filled the air. In two shakes of a lamb's tail, she was off towards Fiskerton, leaving a swirl of cold air in her wake. Our two guests were every bit as impressed as we were. I had made two converts to the cause. As we retraced our steps to the cars, our companions enthused about what an impressive sight the Hall had made and how they hadn't seen a steam engine on the main network for half a century.

I had got my fix and had spread the word, so I felt quite chuffed. I did not drag them out into sub-zero temperatures for the return journey, but Chris and I went down to Fiskerton to see Rood Ashton Hall on her way back to Tyseley. Night time experiences are something else again. My gaze is always drawn to the glow from the firebox, especially noticeable if the firebox door is wide open. I love the way the red glow from the flames lights up the cab, dances on the paintwork and flickers on the smoke and steam.

When I had travelled into the city along this same route in 2018, I had taken exception to the amount of rubbish that had been dumped at the lineside, once the built-up area had started to close in. Basically, it appeared that whatever was on the other side of your garden wall didn't matter as long as it was out of sight. The fact that the other side of the garden wall was the railway was obviously not of the slightest concern to the rubbish dumpers. I had tried to take a photo of it but failed, so my unofficial survey and my wittering about it continued as Nottingham station grew gradually closer.

I really don't like fly tipping, fast food junk on roadside verges and chewing gum splodges on pavements. Yet, in the overall hierarchy of human misdemeanours, these are surely way down the list, so why do they get to me so much? I think it's because they are so obviously in your face and although they may be comparatively minor offences, they represent such inconsiderate and unsociable acts. The railways are in the firing line here, too, and I noticed that there was plenty to complain about in Nottingham's eastern suburbs. Cuttings seem to be the worst. I suppose that once tipped in a cutting, the evidence is immediately out of sight at street level - but not from a passing train!

If there is a footpath parallel to the top of the cutting, it attracts more casual waste and the offenders could have come from anywhere. What strikes me most is where a back garden is separated from the top of the cutting by a single fence, meaning that only the house-holder at that particular property could realistically have dumped the stuff. There are some hideous examples. No need to go to the tip, just heave unwanted items over the fence. Why bother with a bin, at all? Amazing - there they lie, the contents of bulging and torn black bin liners, slowly rotting alongside an old mattress and discarded hardware items, a presentation for passing rail passengers but below the line of sight of the perpetrators, who can continue to enjoy lounging around in their litter-free garden on a pleasant summer's afternoon. I imagine that they may have a few more flies to put up with than their neighbours, though.

I'm a bit more ambivalent about graffiti. I thought for decades that it was just a bad thing. Then along came Banksy and those trying to emulate him. That is so clever, I am drawn to admit. I'm also very much in favour of public art even though it is not uniformly pleasing. Expansive factional murals in Belfast have now become tourist attractions, which we (comfortingly) viewed from an organised bus tour.

Protecting the railway environment is the responsibility of Network Rail and the train operating companies. In 2012, the travel author, Bill Bryson, spearheaded an initiative by the Campaign to Protect Rural England, encouraging the authorities to be more proactive in this respect. Aided by a range of environmental groups at a local level, there will have been many improvements since then but I bet you won't have to travel far by train from your home station to see that plenty more still needs to be done. In the end, as they say, it is down to education.

Looking positively ahead, rather than down at the trackside, the 9.54 to Nottingham took the scheduled 16 minutes from Lowdham to get to there and quite a bit of that was spent at two signal stops outside the station. The Class 170 was warm and welcoming, the décor bright and clean and there were few other travellers around. Those present were reminded via the telecom system that masks were still compulsory, even after yesterday's government announcement that that directive would cease a week from now and that the other Plan B measures had been withdrawn with immediate effect. He went on to tell us exactly how we should be wearing them, to completely cover both mouth and nose. Such advice has either not been sufficiently forthcoming before during this epidemic, it has seemed to me, or it has often simply fallen on deaf ears. "A bit late now, mate", I thought. Generally speaking, however, there is more of a feeling of optimism about Covid at the moment - a dawning that the worst really might now be over with such a large proportion of people in the UK carrying antibodies, either from previous infection or vaccination. This is in spite of continued significant numbers of new infections (still over 100,000 on the day of travel), hospital admissions (1,905) and deaths of those with the disease (330) - although a proportion of this number had Coronavirus but actually died of something else.

In addition to Nottingham's main station, there are lots of other reminders of Nottingham's railway history to explore. In 2016, my daughter took us as her guests for a swim at her gym complex. It is quite a posh affair, compared to the local authority run centre that we usually use, and it appears to attract a lot of young professionals, encouraging those on their way to and from office jobs in the centre of Nottingham to include a daily work-out into their busy routines. It occupies the former train shed of the original Great Northern Railway station.

The Grade II listed building dates from 1857, when it opened as London Road station. It was designed by a local architect, Thomas Chambers Hine. It became the terminus of the line built from Grantham in 1850 by the Ambergate, Nottingham, Boston and Eastern Junction Railway. The ANB&EJR approached the city from Netherfield, a bit further down the Trent valley to the north east. The station had seven platforms which certainly seemed generous, as it was to remain the least well used of the 3 main line Nottingham stations. The frontage is of red brick with an elegant porte-cochere, to accommodate horse-drawn carriages, so that well-to-do passengers could avoid the rain when making their transfer. I was struck on this latest trip back just how pleasing the overall design is, how intricate the finishing off was of some of the ornate patterned brickwork, with balustrades, stone archways, columns and even a bit of crowning ironwork. It was meant to be very imposing and must surely have succeeded in doing that, both in its day and ever since. The later provision of an island platform at London Road High Level, situated on a spur from the Grantham line which threaded its way across an already heavily built-up area of the city to join the Great Central Railway at Weekday Cross, meant that the original building then became London Road Low Level, though the two stations shared a forecourt. The platform for High Level was positioned on two viaducts, separated by a lattice girder bridge over London Road and an adjacent bridge over the Nottingham Canal. High Level survived until the 1960s but the main low-level station had already closed to passengers in 1944. It then operated as a goods depot up to 1972 and for parcels until total closure in around 1989. Damaged by fire in 1996, it was finally converted into the health club.

When - some years ago now, admittedly - I felt that I had needed to build in some variety to my exercise regime, I chose forty lengths as I was forty at the time, though I have consistently kept it just there as I've got older. Swimming is quite boring after a bit and forty has always seemed like plenty. I sometimes imagine myself swimming across the River Mersey estuary, a kilometre across at its narrowest point - facing Egremont Promenade in Wallasey, just to while away the time. That might sound a bit arbitrary, but I suppose it was stock-in-trade for a former geography teacher who had taught on Merseyside.

Managing to avoid the super-tankers and ferry boats once again, I completed my normal forty lengths. On our way out, my daughter informed me that because of the need to work within the limitations set by the framework of the protected building, the swimming pool was actually one metre short of the normal 25. Consequently, this meant that I had not actually managed my regular "nice round number" of a one-kilometre swim, and that I was, in fact, exactly forty metres short. Only by returning for another couple of minutes, would I have given my body what I consider to be its rightful work-out. There was no chance of that happening. I had just thought I had been in particularly good form, making excellent time as I sliced impressively through the waves. Actually, this same daughter has pointed out to me on more than one occasion that my swimming style is nothing if not amusing. She then mimicked the way she says that I stretch my neck and strain my head upwards as if it were on a stalk, so that I don't get any water in my mouth, nose or ears, in what just about passes for a weak breast stroke.

The four broad swimming lanes in the main pool must roughly coincide with the former platform roads in the old station and as I powered down the straight, I could easily have been following the line of a former platform edge. With my head raised, as described, I could clearly see the dagger boards, reconditioned for sure, but still attached to the canopies running the full length of the train shed with the arched former entrance over the tracks themselves ahead of me. Looking from below, the roof itself is an uncovered timber structure, which again appears to be in first class condition, and is clearly in keeping with the overall design as it must have appeared over one hundred and fifty years ago.

Alongside the pool at the station building end is a very chunky cast iron pillar, obviously structural, that reminds me of similar, substantial, weight-bearing columns located at the wharf side in the restored Albert Dock complex in Liverpool. Smaller pillars opposite hold up patterned wrought iron work, now separating large sheets of glass. A hefty and carefully restored red brick wall runs parallel to the adjacent smaller family pool, in the direction of the main station building.

Well, don't you think that is just a great way to preserve an old building? It is still there, tastefully developed and carefully looked after. There are clues everywhere you look as to its former use and plaques to help the mystified to make sense of what has been going on there all this time. It is protected for future generations, fulfils a useful role in the modern city and provides work for local people. I hope it all lives happily ever after. The next time I went for a dip, I promised my body that I would complete 1040 metres, to make up for the restriction forced on me last time by Mr Hine.

However, railway heritage in Nottingham is not all about its former stations. At Netherfield there was a vast triangular layout of lines and sidings, at the heart of which was Colwick sheds. I had underlined 40E Colwick in my 1962 combined volume, telling me that I must have been there once before, many decades ago, but unusually, I couldn't remember anything about it at all. It must have been right at the end of things, when the building still stood, but the rail action had all gone. Anyway, in May 2016, here I was again, walking around the same bit of ground, but all totally unrecognisable.

I hate shopping. My perfect shopping trip, when I have finally been persuaded that I can no longer do without a certain new article of clothing, because I "look so tatty I don't want to be seen out with you anymore", is a quick visit to a high street outfitters of no more than ten minutes duration, followed by half an hour roaming round a bookshop, followed by lunch out, an hour in an art gallery, then home. That immediately gets the painful bit out of the way, after which, it falls neatly into the "now it's just a day out" category. My cunning plan sometimes falls foul of Chris's ability for lateral thinking.

In practice, this means that she may have stated that her aim is to make only one or two purchases, but when actually surrounded by all that stuff, she goes off at a tangent and identifies all sorts of household items which were definitely not on the list she showed me - the proof I had required to see before our departure that we were embarking on a trip of limited duration.

Even worse than the city or town centre shopping expeditions are the out-of-town retail outlets, where there is nowhere nice to eat and I also find that I have landed in a cultural desert. This latest example we drove into is called Victoria Retail Park in Netherfield, on the edge of Nottingham. I just wished I was somewhere else, or maybe, in this instance, the location was actually OK, but it is just that time has changed it.

While my wife checks out that her latest bit of communications gadgetry is available, I sit on a bench and look after the shopping bag. I close my eyes and whisk myself back more than fifty years. Of course, I've been here once before. The ex-Great Northern Railway motive power depot on the flood plain of the River Trent at Colwick was one of the very few Eastern Region sheds that I ever reached but it was like a ghost town by the time I finally got there. If only I had got there just a decade before that. I comforted myself with that notion, smelling the sulphurous smoke, listening to the clanking from the worn bearings and connecting rods on the ancient, overworked freight engines moving around the extensive yards, where I was now sitting.

There would have been ex-LNER locomotives in large numbers, but few namers amongst them. That would have upset me at the time, I thought. These were just black and grubby. Many of them were different, however, and lots of them had prominent handrails attached to the boiler cladding and wrapped around the smokebox, which also made them stand out from what we were used to. I decided that B1s were not as easy on the eye as our own Black Fives and although the Robinson 2-8-0s were impressive, they looked like a very old design when compared to the Stanier 2-8-0s that we saw all the time. They certainly all had rarity value, for me, though. I would have copped virtually everything I saw and it would have been a good haul.

I was suddenly jolted back into the present. Quite a well-spoken voice enquired, "Have I got to smack your leg in front of all these people?" Choosing to interpret this firstly as a rhetorical question if it was directed at me, and then realising that it was probably more likely to be the infant who just happened to be adjacent to me at that moment, I thought it best to maintain my silence. My principles took another hit instead. I could at least have tried to take a bit of the heat out of the situation with a well-timed merry quip.

I still feel the guilt from the two occasions that I can remember when I smacked my own children, having not just lost patience, but all reason and self-control in the flicker of an eye and as a result of total exasperation and probably over next to nothing. I remember turning round again from my driving seat seconds later to see the red, raised, finger-shaped marks on the thigh of my slight, delicate and dumbfounded daughter, sitting strapped into the back seat of the car, sandwiched between her, no doubt, equally guilty brother and sister, too shocked even to cry, as a result of my uncharacteristic lapse. The sickening wave of remorse hit me as though I had been jettisoned down a chute into boiling water. It stays with me to this day. I still keep apologising to her for it.

I had completely lost it at the time, but this parent in the here and now was actually making a calculated, premeditated decision as to a violent intervention and had very publicly brought passers-by into the equation for a bit of added humiliation. It sounded very much like official parental policy, in this case. At least, I could have claimed to have had the intention of not hitting my children. Instead, I made every effort to return to my hazy memories of Colwick shed, embellished by my fertile imagination. Before any more threats of violence were directed at any other very small people nearby, I persuaded my wife to call it a day.

In fact, we had dropped in at Colwick and Toton on our way back from Grantham youth hostel, where we definitely stayed the night on the 10th of April 1969, less than a year after the end of steam on BR and a year before 40E, by then re-coded 16B, was finally closed. I had actually decided not to list any details of trips we made between the end of steam and 1970. This was my personal protest at steam's demise - my one-man campaign, which, as you might have noticed, fell on deaf ears and was completely overlooked by the authorities.

All that remained of Colwick's railway past until recently was the London Midland Railway Club Association's meeting place in the building that was formerly the staff canteen. That has now disappeared as well to be replaced by a modern fast-food outlet and there is a supermarket at the former shed site on the other side of the main road that has subsequently cut a swathe through the whole area.

The next time you are "encouraged" to go shopping there, try and grab a quiet moment and let your mind drift back to what it was like there sixty years ago. It's easy, apparently. I can only hope that you are brought back down to earth gently. I believe we are all a bit vulnerable when we are emerging from a hypnotic trance. I hope there is no big bully there to spoil the moment for you.

On the other side of the city in May 2018, I recorded that my grandson - and my passenger, on this occasion - was 18 weeks old and therefore oblivious, for the time being anyway, of the history of the track formation directly ahead of his current method of transportation.

With luck, Grandad will explain all in the fullness of time. The pram driver's view is of the old Great Central Railway in its approach to the city of Nottingham from the south. We are adjacent to Ruddington Lane, Wilford and at the site of former bridge 295, looking north. That there is an up line and a down line in place along the formation today is, of course, courtesy of the soon to be opened extension to the Nottingham tramway system, as it threads its way out from the city centre to the south westerly margins at Clifton.

The impressive, four-track, GCR River Trent viaduct (bridge 289) and the Nottingham South Goods signal box, which once commanded the approach to that crossing just to the north of here, are long-gone.

Looking south from the Ruddington Lane tram crossing in the direction of former bridge 296, the GCR alignment went straight ahead. The modern tram tracks are crossed by the A52, the Nottingham southern ring road, before veering off to the right towards Clifton. A little further on, is the Great Central Railway (North), well established in the old ordnance depot at Ruddington. With the replacement of the missing link over the ex-MR main line at Loughborough under way, the dream of a reinstated Leicester to Nottingham intercity steam railway is closer to becoming a reality.

There is plenty of time for my companion to learn about the erstwhile sights and sounds along the route of the Master Cutler and the South Yorkshireman that might have attracted his attention at his current abode, had he arrived there a few generations earlier.

Walking the "buggy friendly" modern footpath alongside the route towards Wilford, I noticed these tell-tale blue bricks forming a small bridge that crosses the stream at the approach to the Compton Acres tram stop, close to the site of former bridge 294. Wilford brick works was on the east side of the line to the south of this point. That area is now occupied by Wilford Industrial Estate, and the surroundings are now engulfed by housing developments.

That urban growth, of course, is what encouraged

the development of phase two of the Nottingham Express Transit (NET) system, with the two newer lines between them more than doubling the network, adding 17.5 kilometres of new route and 28 more tram stops. The second line passes Queen's Medical Centre above ground, then on via Nottingham University and Beeston before ending up at Chilwell.

I never travelled on the former GCR in BR days. I didn't go around Annesley or Woodford Halse sheds, nor did I ever go trainspotting on any of its stations. It was an unknown quantity to me, sandwiched between the West Coast Main Line, which we knew very well from our regular visits to Crewe and Preston and the East Coast Main Line, a route that we held in high esteem as a kind of enthusiast's El Dorado. The GCR occupied the railway shadowlands of my youthful imagination, sandwiched between the two. Like the S&D and the Waverley route, it was gone before I had a chance to pay it the attention it deserved.

Living in the East Midlands today, I'm very conscious of the course of the old GCR, both in areas where it has left no trace and those where the blue brick infrastructure still provides an indicator of former glories. Until relatively recently, in addition to the Nottingham Victoria clock tower that somewhat incongruously overlooks the entrance to the shopping centre of the same name, there were many other clear reminders of how, rather belatedly at the end of the nineteenth century, the GCR had cut a remorselessly straight north to south path right through the middle of a built-up area.

Weekday Cross was the best known of these locations, now immortalised in the work of Guild of Railway Artists member, Rob Rowland, amongst others. I found its distinctive name and its unconventional, yet instantly recognisable, railway location intriguing. Photographs of it must have appeared in Trains Illustrated and elsewhere with some regularity in the 1960s. The elevated junction, hemmed in amongst the cityscape, was formed where the east-to-north spur from the former Great Northern Railway's route to Grantham joined the GCR. As the name suggests, this area was actually at the heart of the medieval city and it has been an important location continuously since Saxon times.

The Contemporary Art Gallery is located on High Pavement and next to Weekday Cross. The Great Central Railway emerged from the south portal of the tunnel beneath the city centre, before crossing the Midland station at right angles and heading towards the bridge over the river. The photo looks south down the stairway that leads to the Broad Marsh. The former junction below still has an imposing original brick-built retaining wall visible, complete with a recess for the permanent way workers.

In July 2017, an exhibition at the Contemporary entitled Absolutely Nothing contained a work by the Italian artist, Lara Favaretto, called "Thinking Head", in which clouds of steam slowly rose from the gallery roof. The accompanying blurb insisted that this vapour is totally uncontrolled by the artist, that it will move in shifting patterns and that "the intensity of the steam clouds above will correspond to the intensity of the thinking happening inside".

I would hazard a guess that Weekday Cross has not seen so much steam as this for over half a century. The Contemporary, itself, though, will no doubt continue to dispense plenty of artistic hot air long after this particular exhibition has moved on.

When my daughter and family moved house in 2018, crossing the city from the south west to the north east and into an area of Nottingham that was quite new to me, I was again provided with opportunities to sniff out the city's railway past. "You could take Little Man to the park", she suggested, as we prepared to look after him for a whole afternoon for the first time. "We'll manage", I replied, stoically, wondering which park she meant and where we would find it.

Woodthorpe Grange Park turned out to be the one in question. "There is a bit of an old railway line there", my wife interjected, having made an earlier foray with the buggy in that direction. My interest aroused, what had started out as a leisurely walk to the park suddenly became a bit of a mission - such is the way for those of us who are that way inclined. "I can smell railways", I had apparently said to my dad (meaning from some distance, of course), when I was only a couple of years older than Little Man. Dad reminded me of it at least monthly, or so it felt, throughout the rest of his lifetime. I didn't mind a bit. I had clearly nailed my colours to the mast at an early age.

The Nottingham Suburban Railway was only three and a half miles long. It ran from Trent Lane Junction, Sneinton, in the south, where it left the Great Northern Railway, to Daybrook Junction in the north where it linked once again to a wider arc on the eastern side of the city, which was part of the Derbyshire and Staffordshire Extension, a route that also belonged to the GNR and subsequently became known locally as the "back line". To the south, the GNR had insisted on a flying junction to cross their existing main line at Trent Lane so that there would be no interference with eastbound traffic. The NSR opened in 1889 and served three local brick-making concerns near Sherwood and Thorneywood, the two short branches east of the line finally reaching the factory sites up rope-worked inclines driven from engine houses.

This part of the city is distinctly hilly, as any seasoned local pram pusher will tell you, and there were no less than four tunnels required during the line's construction. The double track formation climbed for two and a-quarter-miles at gradients of up to 1 in 50 before dropping down towards Daybrook at 1 in 70. The tunnels were interspersed with the three intermediate stations of Thorneywood, St Ann's Well and Sherwood. The hope was, as the title of the line suggested, that the railway would attract workers in their daily commute to the city centre from these expanding residential areas.

Circumstance dictated otherwise. In 1900, the Great Central Railway opened their line into Victoria station and took away much of the NSR's passenger traffic from the northern outskirts. Its importance was further reduced by the establishment of an electric tram service close to all three of its stations in the years that followed, a network which also made its way into Nottingham city centre past Victoria station.

As a result, all three NSR stations closed in 1916 and it became a through route only for passenger trains, thereafter, in addition to the sparsely operated pick-up freights and the brick works wagons. In 1923, the independent NSR (though it had actually been run by the GNR, by agreement, up until that time) became part of the LNER. The line was singled in 1930. It was severed at the Trent Lane end by an enemy bombing raid in 1941 and was never re-connected. Freight ended in 1951 and the last passenger service to pay a visit was an enthusiasts' special, via Daybrook, in 1954. That was followed by the dismantling of the track, which was eventually completed three years later.

Woodthorpe Grange Park occupies the grounds of the former family home of Henry Ashwell. It was built in 1874 and is now a Grade II listed building. Though compensated when the NSR cut a swathe both across and beneath his estate in 1889, and in spite of having had a tunnel named after him, Ashwell decided to sell the property - to Edward Parry, no less - who was the designer and the chief engineer for the railway in the first place. By 1905, Parry had sold it on again, to a local councillor called Godfrey Small. In 1922, it opened as a public park, finally having been purchased by Nottingham City Council. In more recent times, it has gained a Green Flag Award, recognising it as a well-managed park and open space as part of a national scheme that was set up in 1996, though, come to think of it, hardly the first time it would have enjoyed the presence of green flags. From the house, now used as council offices, we wandered down the slopes that had made the digging of Ashwell's tunnel a necessity. Both the former portal sites are fenced off and the material that had been dumped to block the tunnel mouths is now covered with mature vegetation. Just outside the park on the south side, blocks of flats occupy the location of the former Sherwood station. The cutting on the approach to the south portal is clearly defined and is currently occupied by a concrete cul-de-sac and a line of garages.

On the north side of the tunnel, a brief section of the former railway's course is just about discernible, with an even shorter section of single-track rail bearing a full-size model of the front end of a steam locomotive. It has been bricked in under the bridge carrying Woodthorpe Drive over the formation, as a sculptured reminder of the old NSR. A cast iron plaque nearby informs visitors about the landscape's history.

I found these discoveries all very interesting, of course, but Little Man did not bat an eyelid throughout our perambulations, in spite of my "off-path" diversions across some fairly rough terrain. "Sleep well, Little Man", I thought. There is plenty of time for railway heritage and for lots of other stuff in between.

I had been reminded how quickly railway landscapes can change on my recent return to Worksop, and so it was again today at Nottingham. What I had previously observed to be a modest stabling and refuelling point east of the station at Eastcroft has become a much more substantial affair with comparatively recent buildings added for maintaining East Midlands Railway's DMU fleet. Next door is another new development including further under-cover provision where Boden Rail now service Colas Rail Class 37, 56 and 70 locomotives.

Having taken the pictures that I had previously had in mind, I was back at Nottingham station with a few minutes to spare for the 10.58 to Newark. The Class 158 unit standing at platform 3b was indicated as such on the VDU, or so I thought. I went to take a photo and returned to find the doors open on the second car.

I put a foot on the step as the high-vis' train operator shouted "Not boarding", at me, before immediately repeating it and now waving his over-sized table tennis bat in my direction. "Not in service", he added, belatedly – maybe having considered that he had sounded a tad abrupt. It was my mistake, of course, but it was an easy one to make. The train doors were open, the illuminated panel at the front end said Grimsby which is in the same direction as Newark, if admittedly a little further on, though the light was flashing on and off, so perhaps that was a clue. The engine was running, the train indicator suggested that the 10.58 was on time and there had been no visible or audible announcement while I was there that this train was not in service or that passengers should stand back from the platform edge. As it crawled out soon afterwards towards the Eastcroft depot, the now late departing Class 170 unit for Newark rapidly took its place at the platform and I finally took my seat.

After we had left Carlton the audio train announcement told us that Lowdham was the next stop. The train immediately slowed and then stopped at Burton Joyce station, though the doors remained closed and no door lights came on. A young lady who had left her seat to stand in the vestibule when she had heard the announcement started to press the button, obviously thinking that the train had reached Lowdham and wondering why the door lights had not become illuminated. "This is Burton Joyce", I piped up. "I think we have just been held up before the level crossing", I added, as helpfully as I could. I reassured her that it really was Lowdham next and that I was alighting there, myself. As we approached our destination, the guard apologised for any confusion he had caused. Who would have thought that a short off-peak journey could have become so problematic? We had also been warned while the train was slowing down that the gap between the train and the platform edge was wider at Lowdham than most, but I was all attention by this stage. I managed it in one leap and without holding onto anything.

6. Loughborough

There it was in black and white on the front of the Loughborough bus. "Town Centre, Train Station". "It's railway station", I had muttered to myself. "Don't be so pedantic", I had replied. "It's railway station", I had repeated. When did that happen, then? Is it an Americanism? Almost certainly. Should it grate with me? Probably not. Language is dynamic. It changes all the time. New words are added to official dictionaries with each new edition. Some words go out of fashion and get dropped. If people reply that they are "good", rather than well, when you ask after their health, is there really any need to grimace? If the youngsters around the table with you at the restaurant ask the waitress, "Can I get a steak?" rather than, "Can I have a steak?", it doesn't mean that they are about to dive into the kitchen and help themselves. Better just get used to it.

Loughborough Great Central train station here we come. Cards on the table – I'd already visited Loughborough by train during this period, and well before my return to the railway for the Winter Steam Gala on the weekend of 28th to the 30th January 2022. With my Great Central Railway volunteer's hat on, I had travelled with Chris on the 7-minute return trip from Quorn and Woodhouse, having parked the car in the station yard. We stood in the brake section of the Mark I composite coach with our masks on in both directions. The Last Hurrah of the 2021 season of events had been well attended. That was on Saturday 20th November, just days before the emergence of the Omicron variant and when we were just getting back into circulation - if somewhat tentatively - after the Delta wave had eased off on its own spread.

Between these two visits to the GCR, just over two months apart, daily reported cases of Covid 19 went from 34,637 to 72,727, daily hospital admissions from 733 to 1,732, totals in hospital from 7,977 to 16,149, and reported deaths within the previous 24-hour period from 116 to 296. At the end of the Coronavirus section on the BBC TV news they often now tag on the rider that not all those who have died will have done so as a direct result of this infection, even though they had been infected by it. True, but may that not always have been the case, though perhaps to a less obvious degree? Omicron is certainly responsible for the difference in the figures, even if it is clearly less lethal, having established itself firmly as the dominant variant during the interim. At the end of January 2022, the news is that the recent reduction in overall numbers has now plateaued. At the same time, treatment of those who contract the disease continues to improve and present death rates are reported to be similar to a those inflicted in a bad flu season. One senses that confidence is gradually being restored, even by those who have been justifiably cautious throughout the epidemic. Two days after the abandoning of mandatory wearing of masks in some settings, the GC Railway was urging their continued use on platforms and trains by messages over the Tannoy and on written notices. A noticeable majority had discarded them already.

We repeated our short journey from Quorn to Loughborough, still masked up and standing in the brake section of the coach on a very busy train. One senses that alongside a belief in the power of vaccination and the antibodies stored up as a result of previous infections, there is now a more widespread determination to get out there and enjoy things again, come what may. It is surely the release of a lot of pent-up frustration at two years already largely lost to the disease. The Saturday of the Winter Steam Gala was very well attended, as these events always tended to be before Covid interrupted things.

This old enamel sign is one of a number on Loughborough Central station adding to the authenticity of the location. Not much of a clue as to any inherent dangers to health there. My friend Ian and I came back from our early trips to France wielding multi-packs of duty-free, king-size Royale cigarettes. They were mild and aromatic and I probably thought that they were a little less harmful than Woodbines or Players No. 6, if I thought about it at all. During my smoking years (mostly, of other people's ciggies) between the ages of 13 and 22, the urge to look cool triumphed over any qualms that I might have had about the possible impact on my well-being. If I'd taken any notice of the Craven "A" advert and carried on smoking, I can confidently say that this account would have never existed, which may or may not have been a good thing.

I like these old reminders of former everyday goods that are no longer, well, every day. We have our own example on our kitchen wall in the shape of a cup and saucer advertising Nectar Tea. One that cropped up at auction a few years ago also caught my eye. It was of a pre-1971, London Transport automatic car park sign. It said, "Two shillings a day, enter free, pay as you drive out". "Enter free? That wasn't free", I chuntered. That was paying on the way out. There was nothing free about it. It was payment taken when you left - like purchasing goods in a shop, after a meal in a restaurant or even at an auction. Some things worked the other way around, so we may have paid for a swim before we jumped in the pool or took our seat in the cinema, but no-one said pay now and you are free to leave after you have had your enjoyment. Why did they need to say "Enter free" at all? We know it wasn't a free car park because it had already said that it cost two shillings a day. Were you supposed to wander around town for a couple of hours thinking, great, this isn't costing me anything as long as I don't go back to retrieve my car from the car park. How cool is this? I'm beating the system. Perhaps I should just stay here longer, as its still free, and just carry-on walking around town some more. In fact, I think I might just leave my car there for ever as

I don't have to pay while it's in there. That way, I just carry on winning. Brilliant, I'll get the bus home instead and use my bus pass - which is also free.

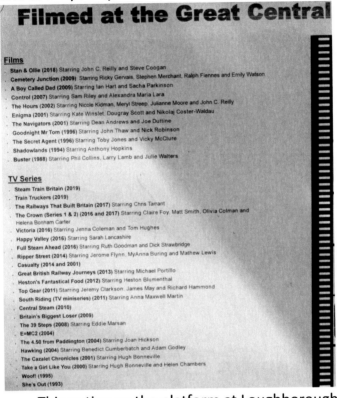

Filmed at the Great Central

Films
- Stan & Ollie (2018) Starring John C. Reilly and Steve Coogan
- Cemetery Junction (2009) Starring Ricky Gervais, Stephen Merchant, Ralph Fiennes and Emily Watson
- A Boy Called Dad (2009) Starring Ian Hart and Sacha Parkinson
- Control (2007) Starring Sam Riley and Alexandra Maria Lara
- The Hours (2002) Starring Nicole Kidman, Meryl Streep, Julianne Moore and John C. Reilly
- Enigma (2001) Starring Kate Winslet, Dougray Scott and Nikolaj Coster-Waldau
- The Navigators (2001) Starring Dean Andrews and Joe Duttine
- Goodnight Mr Tom (1996) Starring John Thaw and Nick Robinson
- The Secret Agent (1996) Starring Toby Jones and Vicky McClure
- Shadowlands (1994) Starring Anthony Hopkins
- Buster (1988) Starring Phil Collins, Larry Lamb and Julie Walters

TV Series
- Steam Train Britain (2019)
- Train Truckers (2019)
- The Railways That Built Britain (2017) Starring Chris Tarrant
- The Crown (Series 1 & 2) (2016 and 2017) Starring Claire Foy, Matt Smith, Olivia Colman and Helena Bonham Carter
- Victoria (2016) Starring Jenna Coleman and Tom Hughes
- Happy Valley (2016) Starring Sarah Lancashire
- Full Steam Ahead (2016) Starring Ruth Goodman and Dick Strawbridge
- Ripper Street (2014) Starring Jerome Flynn, MyAnna Buring and Mathew Lewis
- Casualty (2014 and 2001)
- Great British Railway Journeys (2013) Starring Michael Portillo
- Heston's Fantastical Food (2012) Starring Heston Blumenthal
- Top Gear (2011) Starring Jeremy Clarkson, James May and Richard Hammond
- South Riding (TV miniseries) (2011) Starring Anna Maxwell Martin
- Central Steam (2010)
- Britain's Biggest Loser (2009)
- The 39 Steps (2008) Starring Eddie Marsan
- E=MC2 (2004)
- The 4.50 from Paddington (2004) Starring Joan Hickson
- Hawking (2004) Starring Benedict Cumberbatch and Adam Godley
- The Cazalet Chronicles (2001) Starring Hugh Bonneville
- Take a Girl Like You (2000) Starring Hugh Bonneville and Helen Chambers
- Woof! (1995)
- She's Out (1993)

This notice on the platform at Loughborough Central station makes an impressive list. Incidentally, if you ever wondered who it was that stuck down the blue-tac fixing the bottom right-hand corner of the map of the original GCR to the table, for the immediate benefit of Dr Ruth Goodman and Alex Langlands, as featured in the BBC's Victorian Railway series, "Full Steam Ahead", and enabling the discussion that followed about Sir Edward Watkin's grand design for an international railway via a channel tunnel, an idea that was realised a century after his time, then I'm able to report that, yes, it was me, actually.

Rolling back the clock even further to nine months previously, when my three-year-old grandson decided it was high time he went on a train, and my granddaughter followed that up with a personal written invitation for us to join them, we were all set to mark the re-opening of the GCR after lockdown restrictions had been partially lifted for a weekend in mid-April 2021. A resplendent Class 9F 2-10-0 No. 92214 City of Leicester arrived at Quorn and Woodhouse to take the family off to Leicester North and back for a leisurely picnic lunch in their own pre-booked compartment. It was ice creams all round on their return, seated outside at the Butler Henderson café. A brief taste of normality had returned.

Winding back a lot further than that, it was on the fourth of June 1963 that I took my one and only trip on the former Great Central Railway main line between Liverpool Central and Sheffield Victoria, via Guide Bridge. It was also an introduction to the distinctive, 1950s-built, electric locomotives that were based at Wath. The route over the Pennines and through the Woodhead tunnel was closed to passenger trains in 1970 and to all traffic in 1981. It was not until we had reached Sheffield Victoria, in time for our connection to Doncaster via Mexborough, that we found out that we had been hauled over the hills by Class EM2 No. 27000 Electra. While we were under the wires, we noted 17 examples of the Class EM1 26000 Class, in addition to Class EM2 No. 27006 Pandora.

I never ventured any further south on the old GCR until well after its post-1970 renaissance. Over the period of our regular visits since then, it has gone from strength to strength with the extension to Leicester North, re-establishment of a double track main line, relaying of the Mountsorrel branch, reinstatement of the four-track Swithland loop, the unique operation of a complete GPO train working at speed, demonstration freights - the wind-cutter set of mineral wagons and a whole train's worth of closed wagons, an award-winning museum, replacement of the bridge over the Midland main line and the realistic prospect of an inner-city link between Leicester and Nottingham. It is an extraordinary success story with obviously much more to come.

It's not just the GCR, of course. In pre-pandemic 2019, heritage railways contributed nearly half a billion pounds a year to the economy, employed 4,000 people full-time, provided something useful to do for an army of 22,000 volunteers enabling the sector to attract thirteen million visitors a year. This is how I saw it in a blog I wrote in 2016....

What professional enterprises the heritage railways have become since steam was first banned from the national network in 1968. I want to thank publicly all the dedicated visionaries and grafters who have made this possible over the years. To begin with, these lines tended to provide rather short trips, on severely truncated routes, in infrequent trains, running to rather sparse timetables. Often with only one engine in steam, I thought myself fortunate if the locomotive was a prized survivor with a proper ex-BR number and not a former industrial tank.

Today, the heritage railways have extended and consolidated to provide a vast range of different visitor experiences, from Peppa Pig to "pigging out" in an indulgent, luxury dining car experience. The Barry scrap yard legends have continued to come off the production line for the second time in their lives and gala days - with the leading players, especially - offer a feast of authentic steam entertainment for enthusiasts and a much wider public. They continue to re-establish former links with the national network where they can, and they have rejuvenated and improved the quality of their infrastructure almost beyond recognition. Inventive marketing strategies bring passengers back to the railways as they used to be.

On the main line, steam still abounds despite recent problems. Nearly half a century after the disappointment of the national ban that accompanied the official end of steam in 1968, we now have a revitalised steam railway scene. The Great Britain roams the country and a range of operators comb the network conceiving new routes and itineraries for steam. I could never have dreamt that I would watch a "streak" pass through Newark at 92 miles per hour, in 2013. Fire risk, engineering works, congested pathways, engine failures, well-publicised mishaps and under-booked trains still lead to postponements and cancellations but fail to dampen enthusiasm and resolve. All this while the national network itself is ablaze with a wide range of liveries and the system is just bulging at the seams with more passengers than it has ever carried before.

My own lean years, as far as steam was concerned, coincided with family and work commitments, so for some time I visited less frequently than I would have liked to, but greatly valued those rare occasions all the same. Our children experienced many a ride behind steam, as we entertained them with Connect 4, Flower Fairies, Star Wars figures, Hula Hoops (the edible kind) and Ribena, huddled around the Formica-topped tables in the Mark 1 open coaches, wiping the condensation from the window and peering out into the damp and gloom of an English half term holiday landscape. My photos of preserved steam are largely the result of such forays into the railway world, as at a busy Midland Railway Centre at Butterley in October 1982. In 1968, I had thought that this kind of scene had gone for ever.

I'm equally pleased that before the age of mobile phones I usually remembered to take my camera with me when we went out to such venues. Digital technology suddenly made the practicalities of railway photography a whole lot easier, assuming you know your way around the various settings on the camera. This, I find, is still work in progress.

7. Lincoln

The weather just didn't know what it wanted to do with itself on the day I went back to Lincoln. On my early morning bike ride, snowdrops had put in an appearance on the grass verges for the first time this year, hanging brightly from their deep green and very determined shoots. The skylarks I'd heard earlier in the week were out in force again, also convinced that spring was on the way. By the time I'd arrived at Newark Castle for the 11.57 to Lincoln, however, sunshine had given way to cloud and there was a stiff breeze swirling around. The 2-car Class 156 unit pulled in on time for the 28-minute journey, at a cost of £4.40 for us oldies.

Waiting on the station, the numbers of passengers was soon into double figures, but with only me in a mask. All the notices to that effect had gone and it wasn't mentioned either when the train was announced. The government's own website recorded 84,053 new cases of Coronavirus on the 4th of February 2022. 1,596 people were admitted to hospital, contributing to a total of 14,634 inpatients and there had been a further 254 deaths recorded in the previous 24 hours. Officially, the situation nationally has stabilised. Anecdotally, we have heard more incidences of people we know contracting Covid but not getting very ill as a result. This week saw an adjustment to the figures to include those reinfected with the disease, though it was not apparent to me why they were omitted previously. If they'd got it, then they'd got it, surely, even if they'd had it before. Nevertheless, the overall trend seems to be very gradually moving in the right direction and one can sense the generally greater sense of relaxation and a consequent dropping of one's guard when out and about. About a third of travellers, at a guess, still wore masks on board, including quite a few of the younger folk. Since my last time out on the trains, Chris and I have been inside our local pub with friends for a couple of hours and taken an evening meal inside a restaurant, both for the first time in two years. I've also noticed that when you meet someone now, Covid is no longer the first topic of conversation, in fact, it might not even be mentioned at all, which is actually very refreshing when you think about how it had dominated affairs for so long.

We rattled over the flat crossing of the ECML and out over the flat lower Trent valley into often - but not completely - flat Lincolnshire. Lack of altitude meant the railway met roads on level crossings more regularly than in more undulating country and many such locations still have their original Midland Railway Italianate-style crossing-keeper's cottages, all now private residences. Tidy farmland gave way to willow and alder carr near Hykeham. This is close to Whisby Nature Park, where we had once been to see and hear nightingales. They won't be back for a while. They'll need a bit more persuading than that offered by the snowdrops and skylarks that spring is on its way. As the brakes took effect, sight of a majestic and imposing Lincoln cathedral swung into view, astride its hill, just to prove that we shouldn't dismiss the whole county as being vertically challenged.

Amongst Lincoln's many attractions are three fine old railway buildings close to the centre of the city, all of which have found new functions, having previously become obsolete. That's in addition, of course, to the current and attractive Lincoln railway station – known as Lincoln Central until as recently as 2019. It was built in 1848 for the Great Northern Railway.

The original 2-track GNR engine shed that served it was east of the existing station. Opened in 1851, it was soon replaced because movements on and off the shed were complicated by the need to regularly close the roads at level crossings, a problem that still affects movement in this part of the city today. The replacement 4-track shed was built in 1875, west of Lincoln Central station at Brayford Wharf, south of Brayford Pool. Brayford Pool was formerly the Roman port and is now a marina. Originally coded LIN, it passed to the LNER in 1923, becoming 40A under British Railways. It closed in 1964, but was then used as a signing on point for drivers up to May 1973.

The old shed building was eventually renovated as a concert venue on what is now part of the Lincoln University campus. As well as the auditorium for live events, there is a bar and the student's union. Still known as the Engine Shed, the façade is unrecognisable as a former locomotive depot, its appearance transformed by a modern extension in steel and glass. Inside, however, the original arched brickwork pattern is visible on two levels. As you try to visualise its former position in a partially lost railway landscape, the Grade II listed East Holmes signalbox, next to the main line westwards out of Lincoln station, helps you get your bearings.

The former Great Central Railway building at Brayford Wharf also catches the eye. It would be hard to miss it, in truth. Built in 1907 as a goods and grain store, it was used as a builder's warehouse in the second half of the last century, before falling into disrepair by 1998. It was rescued by a £5,000,000 renovation and converted into the main library for the University of Lincoln, opening in 2004.

Lincoln St Mark's station was opened by the Midland Railway in 1846 and closed by British Rail in 1985. Its services were diverted into Lincoln Central, instead. It had actually only been known as St Mark's since 1950. A new chord was constructed to connect the station to the Newark Castle line. After lying derelict for some years, the main station building with its classical-style portico was incorporated into the development of a new shopping centre. On a previous winter-time visit and from the warmth of the coffee house opposite, we admired the glowing honey-coloured stone of the station façade on the other side of the now pedestrianised station approach road. The barista also warmed to his task, whilst simultaneously ruing the changes already underway in the nature of high street retailing – and that was pre-pandemic.

On my return, I wandered along to St Mark's, only to find that the barista's concerns for our town and city centres had indeed been realised, but closer to home than he might have imagined. St Mark's station's former retailing occupants have gone and the building is locked up. Notices in the windows show that it is currently for let. Though the coffee shop survives as part of a successful chain, footfall on the pavement outside is likely to be less than before until new tenants can be attracted to the wonderful old building facing it.

Back at Lincoln's current station, things were looking decidedly busier. The 5-car bimodal Azuma unit would be depending on its own diesel engines to reach the overhead wires at Newark Northgate. Quite a crowd had gathered for the 13.24 departure with the promise of first class accommodation at the front of the train, as well as an "at your seat" refreshment service, on the journey to King's Cross. Units also sped off to Sheffield and Leeds, Nottingham and Leicester, Spalding and Peterborough and Grimsby in less than an hour. Three Class 66 hauled freights carried containers and cement through the centre roads during the same period.

An elderly gentleman seated on platform 4 suddenly sprang to his feet, temporarily abandoning his half-eaten sandwich to scurry towards the platform end to join three other guys all with cameras trained on the latest Class 66 to pass through eastwards. "Don't get in the way", he instructed me, as I belatedly made it in time to share the moment. I took a step to the side, which luckily was enough to keep him onside. A local bell ringing practice struck up, which also seemed very apt in this characterful cathedral city.

The university at Lincoln has expanded steadily over the years, including the provision of a number of new buildings in the former railway territory close by. Many of the students were now heading home on this Friday afternoon, thus making my own train homewards a bit more problematic than I would have liked. As I waited for my train, the station announcer politely requested that we should use a face covering if we can "as a courtesy to other travellers", which I thought probably caught the mood appropriately of these ever-changing times.

I was quickly on board when the train pulled in and I sat down next to a window on the back seat in the carriage and hoped everyone else would walk past me. The coach filled up and a lady roughly my age with a mask on sat next to me until Hykeham. I had chosen the right side, though, because as we accelerated away from that station stop, we passed a large bird of prey, quartering about two metres above a meadow of rough grassland, moving very deliberately, head down, tail flicking and alongside the train, but all too dark and fleeting for an accurate identification. For a few moments I stopped worrying about keeping safe. Then two people further down the coach started coughing in unison.

8. Tamworth

Tamworth was special in the days of steam. I knew all about it but I never went there. My love affair with the West Coast Main Line did not even start with Crewe or Preston, though as we were based on Merseyside both would soon become regular haunts. My introduction to the WCML was actually at Warrington. Our visit there in October 1960 was almost certainly the first purposeful trainspotting trip that I ever went on as part of a group. I was eleven years old. During my first half-term holiday at big school, the railway society planned a day out for us on Bank Quay station. We travelled to Warrington Central on the old Great Central Railway route from Liverpool Central High Level. I clearly remember walking along the approach road to Bank Quay and being welcomed by Coronation Pacific Class No. 46223 Princess Alice in green livery, standing at the down platform waiting to depart and most likely bound for Glasgow. Who would have thought that there was so much fun to be had in the shadow of an enormous soap factory? Warrington may not have been pretty but I have loved that particular moment ever since. I even have an original painting on my office wall showing a panoramic view of activity at the station by the prominent railway artist, John Harrison.

Meanwhile, and somewhat further south, what was special about Tamworth was that the WCML was crossed at this point by the ex-Midland Railway from Derby to Birmingham, a major route for cross-country traffic between the north east and the south west of England. Its other big attraction was an accessible field that permitted good views of both lines. That was situated just east of the station on the south side of the tracks. A meeting place for local spotters, many of whom remember it with great affection, it now supports an estate of chalet bungalows.

The plan I have in mind as 2022 unfolds is, firstly, to up the regularity of my trips out. Secondly, I'm going to concentrate my activities on days when my wife is also out for lunch. This should not be too difficult. Chris has a very active social life, much more so than my knees will currently allow for me. She goes for long walks with a group of friends both locally and in Derbyshire, runs with a friend early on Saturday mornings, plays golf, badminton (for which she is also the club treasurer) and tennis (including matches, home and away, for both clubs), goes swimming (for which I sometimes join her), attends art lectures as a member of The Art Society's Nottingham branch, visits art galleries with another friend, participates in a spoken French class, volunteers in Sherwood Forest with the RSPB, picks up our grandchildren from school once a week, performs all the necessary tasks in the garden apart from cutting the grass, keeps the bird feeders stocked up and takes an active part in a shared community allotment. That is in addition to various occasional coffee and lunch dates. You can see why a lunchtime together is generally welcomed, if only in granting an opportunity for a catch-up, when I can tell her all about my time on the computer and the highlights from my daily bike ride. We are like ships in the night.

Though I have never stood on Tamworth station before, the name of the town is very familiar. As a service station on the M42 motorway, it is just the right distance from home for my necessary mid-morning pit stop when driving towards the south west, which we have often done. It is just on the approach to Tamworth that my diuretic pill usually kicks in and I start fidgeting in my seat. "Do you need the loo?", I am asked, and we turn off and find that Tamworth services is always there to oblige.

This time, however, I thought I'd sample Tamworth as a convenient way of catching up with what was happening on the WCML. Burton-on-Trent station is 58 minutes from home by car down the A38. This allowed me to maintain the pattern that I began with my visit to Doncaster and have maintained since, namely, a short train trip while Covid infection rates are still too high for comfort, even for the fully vaccinated. Arriving at my eventual destination by train rather than just travelling throughout by car usually makes car parking less problematic. I can generally find street parking more easily near a smaller station and I also feel I have more of a right to be at my destination as a fully-fledged, if rather miserly, rail user. I don't have to explain my presence when entering or leaving the station of my choice and I cut down on unnecessary contact with others, into the bargain. Policies towards station access keep on changing, it seems to me. Are there barriers or no barriers? Some locations had previously fitted them only to take them away again. Are tickets inspected on crossing the threshold between concourse and platform? Are tickets swallowed up by the machine or can I keep them as a reminder of my journey? Are platform tickets still issued, or is there open access for all? There is no need to worry about any of this if you already possess a ticket to ride.

No sooner had I ventured to Worksop than the Omicron variant really took off. "What am I worried about?", you might ask. After all, we've both received three jabs, as recommended, and we have been operating our own plan B throughout the pandemic in terms of wearing masks in public places, hand hygiene and keeping our distance. We have proceeded with caution, not just because of our age but because we carry other conditions that could work against us if we got ill. We just don't want to take unnecessary risks, yet we want to take as active a part in society as we can. Effectively this means taking control of our own movements and avoiding situations where we think that control might not be possible, for whatever reason. So it was that after the Worksop trip another pause was required while the full extent of the Omicron wave became clear. Though leading to a milder illness, it was certainly very infectious and the rapid spread over the holiday period was soon followed by a doubling in hospital admissions – firstly of the young and largely unvaccinated, but soon followed by older folk like us, many of whom had been inoculated but had apparently been dragged down by other factors. We needed to sit tight for a bit longer whilst it hopefully started to blow over, which it is now showing signs of doing. On the day of my Tamworth visit there were 102,292 new infections, 1,399 people were hospitalised, meaning there were then 16,594 inpatients with Covid, and there were sadly another 346 deaths recorded since the previous day. Rates may have stabilised but it's hardly gone away. Perhaps it never will.

I drove to Burton-on-Trent station. I found it perched on top of a hump-back bridge. At first glance, it looked like someone's fairly substantial brick-built shed. I had seen online that there was a station car park, but where was it? It was not visible from the station approach. The very limited number of parking spaces marked out on either side of the hut appeared to be for staff use only. There was just one space visible that was clearly demarcated for someone in possession of a disabled sticker for their car. I wandered off past plenty of dowdy, closed-down former shops and tried to extricate myself from one-way streets and bus-only lanes in search of some on-street parking within comfortable walking distance of the station for someone with two bad knees and a bad back but no disabled sticker.

The 11.21 to Tamworth, one of the now seemingly

ubiquitous Class 170 units, was too busy for comfort so I stood next to the door for the 11-minute journey, at a cost of £5.00 with a railcard. The lady on the opposite side of the gangway had the same idea for keeping her distance. She commented on the morning's welcome sunshine, contrasting it with the two unremittingly heavy grey days that had preceded it.

"I'm changing at the next stop", she offered, adding, "I avoid Birmingham at all costs". I wondered what Birmingham might have done to upset her, but was not tempted to ask. Maybe she just didn't like New Street station's crowded, narrow, sub-terranean platforms with an uncomfortably low roof, in which case I think she had a point. Her distaste for Birmingham meant that she was travelling from Burton to Northampton, via Tamworth and Rugby. I fought for a moment with my mental map of the railway network in the English Midlands, before concluding that that was probably quite logical, and that perhaps Birmingham shouldn't even have been part of the equation in the first place.

I got off at the next stop, too, and made my way downstairs to the down platform on the WCML. Tamworth station opened in 1839 on the Birmingham and Derby Railway, a forerunner of the Midland Railway. When the London and North Western Railway arrived in 1847, a new station was built below the higher-level Midland lines. The cross-country line spans the WCML at right angles, but the north to west chord that used to physically link the two routes was closed in 1969. The station's location was especially important in the post-war years for transferring overnight mail, with special lifts installed to facilitate the operation between the two main lines.

I stood at the London end with the sun on my back and decided it was warm enough to do without a hat, choosing instead a modest intake of vitamin D. There were three much younger railway enthusiasts sharing the space with me. Directly behind us all was the famous old patch, where youngsters just like them had stood and watched some sixty years ago now - and probably many more before that. What struck me most, apart from their undoubtedly keen appetite for trains, was their depth of knowledge about the current system and its workings. I was marginalised to the fringes of the conversation in no time. They were managing very well without me and I thought I'd only embarrass myself if I got something wrong, so I just let them get on with it and wandered off.

The former LNWR lines are four-track through the station, as the platforms serve the two loops. British Railways demolished the original station buildings and rebuilt them in 1962. It is described as having a functional style. The typical 60s architecture and building materials used as part of the modernisation programme have not stood the test of time particularly well, both here and elsewhere and in spite of some subsequent titivation. I decided that Tamworth station is actually awful, aesthetically. I was unable to identify any redeeming features. The platforms are narrow and you are urged to walk along an even thinner strip on the landward side of the bold yellow line. A lack of seating may be in recognition of the restricted available space on the down side, as the opposite platform has some.

The buildings are in the form of a series of boxes for lifts, stairs, waiting rooms and concourse. I went outside into the car park but could not find an elevated position of safety to take a photo of its best side. It doesn't have one. The main entrance has a corrugated iron roof, pitched at a shallow angle. It looks like a factory unit on an industrial estate. Pendolinos, some with very colourful paint schemes, whizzed by, north and south, and an elderly preserved Class 86 made its way from Lichfield to Rugby, between rail tour duties.

A Class 88, No. 88006 Juno, moved south on one of a series of freights, and I failed to stop any of them satisfactorily because I forgot to change my camera setting to "sports mode". Will I ever learn to do these simple things properly? Local services on the WCML were provided by London Northwestern Railway Class 350s, including No. 350253 heading towards Rugby from Crewe.

I had soon had enough of modern Tamworth. The train back to Burton was also sufficiently well used for me to feel obliged to stand at the end of the carriage again and so I stared out briefly onto Britain's green and pleasant land. I've actually never been totally at home in the countryside, I admitted. There are too many animals for a start, like the herd of over-inquisitive cows that had ganged up on us as we made for the only gated escape route from their field. Then there was the horse that tried to bite my elbow when I had finally found the nerve to take a short cut across his patch at Tregaron (We were looking for red kites in the years before the red kites came to us). Instead, he took a piece out of my jumper. Two potentially killer sheep once barred our way in a very confrontational manner on a hillside path just down the road from home. Part of me feels that we are often unwelcome guests anywhere near farmland and especially in those coveted pockets of woodland where they kill birds for fun. The conclusion I've drawn is that the countryside is best viewed from a safe distance and my preferred mode of transport for such forays will always be the railway. Railways provide the opportunity to enjoy pastoral landscapes in comfort and to be protected from rural uncertainties as well as the vagaries of the weather and over-crowded roads. The mosaic of rural Britain is undeniably varied and beautiful, but that pattern - sculpted by nature and then fashioned by man for a further few thousand years to put the finishing touches - unfolds perfectly in the panorama provided through a carriage window, or even, as in this instance, whilst standing in a doorway with my head pressed against the glass.

I reached my car, parked mid-way between the bolted doors of the town hall and a rather imposing church. Two men were standing at the road side on opposite corners as I crossed it. "What are you doing over there, Dave?" one shouted. "Standing in the sun, keeping warm", replied the man clinging on to one of those very flimsy looking unmarked blue plastic bags, with not much in it. I got the impression that standing around, avoiding shadows and generally mooching along on Burton's streets was something they were fairly used to doing. Eight degrees of near warmth, a light breeze and bright sunshine in mid-January were not to be sniffed at, as I'd already discovered.

As I finally dropped down into the shallow valley in which our village snugly fits, free from derelict factories and boarded up shops, I was reminded how lucky I am to live here. I can feed myself as I wish, I don't have to worry too much (yet) about increasing energy bills, and I'm still able to waltz around the country like this, amusing myself on a whim. When it clouded over later in the same afternoon, I wondered what Dave and his mate might be doing next, now that the sun had given up for the day. I hoped that they also had somewhere to go. Chris had been at home for lunch while I was out, between French and golf. I was later reassured that she had managed OK without me on this occasion.

9. York

Off we go again - and with grandchildren in tow this time for a trip on the Azuma to the National Railway Museum. The King's Cross to Edinburgh Waverley on Friday 11th February 2022 was pretty busy by the time it left Newark Northgate, promptly, at 9.46 - or 8.46 as the old Potts clock would prefer to call it. Our first move was to politely ask the two young ladies occupying our pre-booked seats to move, so that we were all able to sit within easy reach of each other round the table, which is important when you are the one in charge of a constant supply of drinks, snacks, magazines, coloured pencils, footballer cards, stickers, plastic figures and other forms of entertainment from the bottomless rucksack.

The illuminated panel above the window on the Azumas makes the old "You're sitting in my seat" routine a whole lot easier to deal with these days. No more arguments over lost reservation cards that might or might not have fluttered to the floor from the little recess above the seat. Each seat's status is lit up for the current stage of the journey, with red for pre-booked and amber for may still be reserved even after the current occupiers have left. They even have a little picture of a window next to one of the two numbers, to discriminate between window and aisle seats.

Many travellers were still in masks and were requested to keep on doing so over the train's P.A. On 11th February 2022, 58,899 new cases, 1,395 hospital admissions, 12,753 in hospital and 193 deaths were recorded for the previous 24-hour period. Since my visit to Lincoln, the government announced that the remaining restrictions about isolating after a positive Covid test would be dropped a month earlier than had been planned. Unless there was an unexpected deterioration in the situation, things should officially be back to normal from the end of February rather than in late March. This was made possible by the scientific data continuing to move in the right direction as far as infection rates and hospitalisations were concerned. The speed at which the disease had retreated more recently was certainly noticeable by the second week in February. Although they still provide a summary at the end of the week, the main evening BBC TV news programme has dropped the daily summaries of the state of play from their bulletins, something they had kept up for the last two years, which also adds to a prevailing mood that this is now fading from the collective consciousness, when compared to some other pressing issues.

My grandson kindly informed me that in order to eat chocolate mini-eggs, I would have to temporarily dispense with my mask, as well. Nor does coffee benefit particularly from any extra filtration provided by an FFP2. My granddaughter looked up from her colouring book to notice that our train was "going really fast", as indeed it had to do to get to York in just three-quarters of an hour from Newark, including a stop at Doncaster.

There were three Direct Rail Services Class 68 locomotives in the station when we arrived at York. Nos. 68016, 68023 and 68034 were distributed between north and south facing bays and an imminent departure for Scarborough. During my recent discussions with young spotters at Tamworth station, I had mentioned that in my opinion the Classes 68 and 88 were the most exciting design since the Western diesels. I was informed that this was because they were made in Spain. They certainly have a bit of razzamatazz about them – a dash of Flamenco or an odd "Ole" or two, posing there in their sharp blue uniforms. No. 68032 was in York station on a previous visit in 2019.

A visit to the NRM with the family is a whole different ball game to my more usual solitary self-indulgent ventures. We spent as much time in the food hall and the play area outside as we did with the exhibits, though the model train layout intrigued for a short while and the miniature train trip round the yard was probably the highlight of the day. How could I possibly have envisaged that as a possible end game, when as a teenager in the 1960s I was wandering around this same bit of ground, then laid out with the tracks serving York North sheds during the last days of steam?

I found time for a quiet moment in Station Hall with the blown-up mural that itemises points of interest in Terence Cuneo's 1967 painting, Waterloo Station, which I learnt had included not only a self-portrait, but his wife sitting in their car, Prime Minister Harold Wilson and even President Charles De Gaulle, in addition to the usual mouse. Nearby are the original George Earl masterpieces, Going North and Coming South, depicting the hunting class at King's Cross and Perth, respectively. The children helped us to identify some of the trophies that the shooting party were bringing back to the capital with them, including antlers, rabbits and red grouse. The tiled map of the North Eastern Railway network was also worthy of closer inspection.

This had been inset day for our local schools and we had therefore been able to pick a day before the hordes that would surely be descending during half term. There were one or two school parties there, too, including a substantial cohort of year three - that's seven-and-eight-year-olds - and all in high-vis' vests. Well martialled by teachers and helpers, they had been very attentive for a short presentation about the Rocket given by a very animated Railway Museum volunteer. I saw the same gaggle having their lunch afterwards on the undercover picnic benches, also in Station Hall. They were doing more talking than eating and it was quite a racket. I love moments like that, because I know I can walk away without a care in the world. It was not always so. Taking kids out of school was always a risk and a massive responsibility, but it was also well worth the effort. Their teacher suddenly stood up, aware of the rising decibels in a public place. "One, two, three!", she shouted. "Eyes on me", they all replied in unison, after which nobody spoke. That's the way to do it, thought I. It was a masterstroke. Why hadn't I come up with that? Mind you, I'm not sure it would have worked quite so well with recalcitrant sixteen-year-old youths.

York is certainly high up on my "love of place" list and I've made many visits there over the years. Going back a bit, to November 2010, the National Railway Museum celebrated World Toilet Day with a feature entitled "Lifting the lid on train toilets". Apparently, shops near main line stations in Victorian times sold medical appliances, then called urinals, for use by passengers on longer journeys. Queen Victoria's "Palace on Wheels", built in 1869 for the London North Western Railway and also on permanent display in Station Hall at the NRM, provided three toilets, one for her majesty, one for her ladies-in-waiting and one for lower class attendants. Unfortunately, the Queen's own loo, described as a period piece in its own right, was positioned over the wheels and the consequent regular splattering made for some unfortunate odours as well as an alternative use for the phrase, "a royal flush". Contemporary toilet matters are more concerned with improving access for all passengers and efforts to reduce unnecessary use of water. Some modern stock employs what sounds like strong hydraulic activity to remove the evidence. Powerful suction springs into life as soon as you go anywhere near the flushing mechanism. Pink chemicals suddenly well up in the bowl and your efforts are hungrily devoured in no time by the noisy poo monster underneath the floor. Apparently, modern systems have either chemical retention tanks or composting toilet tanks, which use biological action to break down the waste before depositing it on the track bed, by way of a chlorine sanitising tank. When pointing Percy at porcelain on a train, which gentlemen can claim they have never wafted a spray across the floor in the smallest room after a sudden jolt over the points, heavy braking for an unexpected signal check or a relatively cavalier switch onto the slow line?

We also reached both versions of the Great Gathering, at York and Shildon in 2013. All six surviving Class A4 Pacifics, including the two temporarily repatriated from America - Dominion of Canada and Dwight D Eisenhower, were on show at both venues. There was a lot of moaning about not being able to get photos of the locomotives because there were too many people straying into the shots. I'm not impressed with this particular whinge. Trains are all about people, as well as machines. That was certainly the nature of the occasion in this instance. It was a celebration to be enjoyed by all – more of a jamboree. There are often separate photographers' viewings, charter trains, high vis' vest wearers' passes for the lineside, special night-time openings and, no doubt, all sorts of other accommodations made for people who really can't countenance other people straying into their view finders. I didn't bother much with photos at either venue. I basked in an event that would never to be repeated, felt honoured to have been able to witness these wonderful locomotives at the head of day-to-day express trains in the early 1960s, relished the company of like-minded friends and just enjoyed the moment.

It had been to celebrate my 65th birthday in the February of the following year that I travelled first class for the first time in my life, via York, on a day trip to Edinburgh. I'd hardly had a chance to sit down before I was offered a cup of coffee. That was nice of him. I could get used to this, I mused, as I settled into my seat. "Wine, sir?" "No thank you" - it was not even mid-day. I chose coffee again, followed by fizzy water. Then came lunch; quiche and salad and all very tasty. "No thanks, no wine". It was still only 12.30. Oh no! A dirty glass for my water, should I complain? They've been so attentive. It would seem so ungrateful. I rubbed it on my napkin. It looked like an ingrained dullness, imposed by an automatic dishwasher. It'll do. Don't want to make a scene. I was only a teacher, you know, I'm not used to being fussed over like this. I bet they can spot us first class virgins a mile off. Too polite, not quite sharp enough in our interactions, not relaxed enough in our demeanour. But I've got this comfy chair and this table all to myself and the views of the Northumberland coast would be even better if that bloke had not chosen, inexplicably, to close his blind. His seat and his prerogative, of course, but do you know what you are missing, exactly?

People do that when they are flying, as well. They get a window seat and promptly shut the blind. Why? There is so much geography out there that I've not seen before and will probably never see again, things I've been going on about for decades on maps in school and here they are in reality, at last. On our recent trip to visit our son and family in Washington DC, I had to walk to the back of the plane and peer through the last little window in the fuselage to see the vast and desolate, ice-stripped Canadian wilderness with its thousands of lakes and an occasional spider's leg of a road trying hopelessly to take a straight course across it all. The flight attendant asked me if I was all right. I muttered something banal and returned to my seat next to the aisle, like I'd just been told off.

I'm not sure I'm entitled to what is effectively a second go at lunch, so when they come around yet again, I politely let it be known that I have eaten already, but that I really fancy a sandwich. "No problem, sir, which one would you like, sir?" No, no wine, thanks (again), but the sandwiches and crisps are excellent and a nice cup of tea is just the job. The truth of the matter is that I'm so unused to being on the receiving end of all this pampering that I'm not quite taking advantage of the opportunity to relax in the lap of luxury, in the way that I had envisaged. Perhaps I'd be better off in standard class after all. Trainspotter, know your place. Mind you, it is quieter in here. People are polite but brief with each other. I sense that one reason many have chosen it is precisely so they do not have to go in for any unnecessary conversation. They occasionally talk in friendly tones to distant significant others by phone, but there is less interaction between passengers and it is purely functional when it occurs. They want to be left alone, making exceptions only to be fairly constantly plied with food and drink. Everybody except me seems deeply focussed on some matter of urgency involving a file, a computer or a mobile phone. I assume it is work related, in most cases. I'm only there as a pleasure seeker, but why do I also feel like I'm a bit of an imposter?

I am very well fed and watered by the time we get to Waverley station, so first stop is the loo. It must have suddenly come over me when I stood up. That can happen these days. "30p? You must be joking?" Off I rush down Princes Street in search of quality at a more reasonable price and find just the place in John Lewis's, always reliable and "never knowingly undersold", whatever that means. On the way back I have an even better seat. Facing and window, the aisle is at its widest here, with only one seat either side of it. I can stretch out as far as I can in any direction without inconveniencing anybody else, though I might look a bit strange if anyone happens to look up from their laptop for a second at that precise moment. I feel totally spoilt. "You deserve this", I tell myself. Think about all those dire, wet, Thursday afternoons with 5C, banging on about communications corridors, for example, as we glide smoothly past all the traffic on the A1 - even the stuff going our way at 70 mph.

Tea is Moroccan chickpea tagine with fruity couscous and harissa. I don't know what tagine is, though I think I've heard of harissa. Oh no, sultanas! I can't leave a hillock of sultanas on the side of my plate in first class. What will they think of me? It's time for a birthday drink and a toast to myself. I choose a can of Continental lager. It's not just cool but triple filtered, so that's a big relief, obviously. I have yet another glance at the antimacassar, just to check that I've not absent-mindedly scratched my head at some stage and left a mark on it.

Another catering crew comes on at Newcastle. They won't know that I've already had a meal, so I could be on for some more food without risk of embarrassment. An extraordinary day ends with further sandwiches and even another cup of tea before I drive myself safely home from the station. My dip into this other world of travel is over for the time being, but I must say that I've enjoyed it immensely. I'm sure I'll get better at it, too; a touch of class and not before time. I didn't bother with any tea that evening, not even a slice of birthday cake. As I recalled to friends on my return, because East Coast Trains had looked after me so well in both directions, I did not spend a penny all the time I was in Scotland, other than at John Lewis's. I might claim that as a first in the Guinness Book of Records - the only visitor to have been in the country for three hours without parting with any cash.

In 2016, the National Railway Museum put on a special display to mark the Flying Scotsman's return to steam after a lengthy, troubled and expensive overhaul. Under the subdued but ambient lighting of the Station Hall Gallery, an imaginative, uncluttered and carefully presented display of her historical importance to the nation was assembled. This followed her momentous and triumphant journey from King's Cross to York in February of that year, when hundreds of thousands of well-wishers crowded the lineside, and some of them got a bit too close for their own safety and for the peace of mind of those trying to run a railway. Taking pride of place at the exhibition put on in her name was a previously unseen gem. The eminent twentieth century painter, Frank Mason, perhaps best known for his maritime scenes, was also commissioned many times by the London and North Eastern Railway and later by

British Railways to provide the art work for posters promoting travel by train to a range of UK locations and most notably to those along the North Sea coast.

The quad royal size poster, "East Coast by LNER It's Quicker by Rail", shows the Flying Scotsman locomotive in her 1930s apple green livery at the head of the crack London to Edinburgh express of the same name, emerging from a tunnel and with the magnificent Northumberland coastline stretching out ahead of her. It is a dramatic and powerful image. Speed and purpose are effortlessly conveyed, as connecting rods and pistons thrash. A red glow from the firebox flickers off the smoke and steam, trapped momentarily inside the tunnel mouth. The express bursts out into golden sunlight as passengers settle back to enjoy the same wonderful coastal scenery that provides the highlight of the identical trip north today. It is a classic, capturing a moment in time with dynamism and poise.

This poster is rare - indeed, it may be unique. It belongs to my friend, John Beck, and it has been in his possession since 1988, when he acquired it from one of the leading specialist auction houses. The Science and Society Picture Library, which houses the national collection on behalf of the National Railway Museum and the other centres within the National Science Museums group, does not have a copy and the representative dealing with the loan arrangements said they had had not seen it before. A poster of the same description, apart from the addition of the word "Route" after "East Coast" in the main title, was sold at a Legbourne, Lincolnshire, auction in May 1999, though the 1988 sale of this particular poster seems to have gone unrecorded other than at the auction concerned. It is certainly a very special survivor. John has had it professionally conserved and backed to linen. This was the poster's first outing in nearly 30 years and that provided an opportunity for it to be much more widely admired and it would not have disappointed.

We had also chosen York to celebrate our 45th wedding anniversary and the 50 years since we first met, in 1967. A boat on the river was just the job for starters – sedate, peaceful and reflective, apart from some inconsequential ramblings from the bridge, via the public address system. What a funny old place this city has become. When we first stayed, decades ago now, it was so quiet – Minster, Shambles and walks along the walls. We could find nowhere open on a Sunday evening – no live music, not even a film to watch. We even struggled to find a welcoming pub! Not anymore, because this warm, summer Saturday was race day, wedding day and stags' and hens' day. The men were all over-dressed and the women often the opposite. The railway station was a deluge of smart suits and colourful dresses, so much so that they had devised a one-way system to empty the trains of their potential merry-makers via temporary ticket barriers, backed up by extra high-vis' staff and watched over by a substantial police presence, in what is normally - and thankfully - an open access station from concourse to platform.

Two other old timers were also imminent arrivals at York station on the same day. The Coronation Pacific, No. 46233 Duchess of Sutherland, was on time and looked to be in fine fettle under the roof in platform five, before making a dignified departure for the seaside at Scarborough. Class A3 No. 60103 Flying Scotsman was late in and was then ignominiously dragged out of the station at the tail end of the formation behind the diesel that was rostered to eventually return the special to London, and before we had had a chance to renew our acquaintance or take a photo.

Fifty years ago, Chris and I were both still at school. Later on, during this Saturday out together in York, a gentleman of similar age to us, but kitted out in full school uniform, including cap and haversack, and with short trousers revealing some rather serious looking varicose veins, passed us on the riverside path leading to the Lendal Bridge and again in the adjacent Museum Gardens. For a moment, it felt like "All Our Yesterdays", but, no doubt, he had his own reasons for dressing up. I know that If I'd worn my hair as long as his wig, I would have been sent home from my grammar school to get my hair cut.

We were not quite finished with the unpredictable, though. Entertainment on our packed evening train southwards was provided by a hen that had become separated from the rest of the brood. In black dress with colourful sash, she spent the journey as far as Doncaster trying to persuade train staff that she had not only lost her ticket but that she really wanted to go to Newcastle. It was not quite clear whether she realised the essential geography of her situation, or if that was all part of an attempted act of obfuscation on her part. The guard wasn't buying into it, either, so in the end she had to!

York keeps drawing us back. A number of places do that - a particular Lake District hotel, a handful of bright yellow sandy beaches in Cornwall, particular coastal stretches in the Western Highlands of Scotland and a regular fix in the capital all fulfil a deep-seated need for a personal association with place. I know people who go back to the same place for every holiday and meet up with the same people each time. I get that, but I also feel driven to explore new places, as well as periodically reinforcing these old ties with favoured locations.

10. Shrewsbury

It appears that as soon as they are able to walk, the young grandchildren often choose to run, instead. I'm sure I was the same. Why walk when you can get there quicker by running? Running adds an additional freedom. I can still get that same buzz when I first get on my bike or (increasingly rarely) I swim into the sea. It's liberating and exhilarating. I ran home alone from junior school, as it was safer than walking. We would run to the park, though maybe walk back after the game. We ran to Goodison Park from Kirkdale station and back again after the match, and we ran to the sheds along the routes provided by Aidan Fuller in his loco-shed directory. If we were shouted at by shed staff for trespassing, we probably ran away, and then tried again a bit later. At Shrewsbury, we did not run soon enough or fast enough and got collared by the foreman. Our names and addresses were taken and we received a serious telling-off. That was the only time we ever got caught. We would normally have run back to the station, but on that occasion, in April 1965, we were halfway through a tour by bike. Nevertheless, what a wonderful care-free pleasure it was to be able to run. Sadly, running is now on hold, while I ponder whether a new knee will really have me running around the place again, or is that just wishful thinking?

When our friends on Merseyside, Ian and Sandra, suggested that we meet up in Shrewsbury, I jumped at the chance to return, but at a comparatively gentler pace. Even better, I thought, we'll park and ride from Wellington to fit in with the pattern I'd already established of a short rail journey to some favourite old haunts.

I had not stood on the platform at Wellington for sixty-three years. In 1956 and again in 1959, we took family holidays at Weir Farm, Cold Hatton, in deepest Shropshire. The nearest station was Ellerdine Halt, on the former GWR Wellington to Market Drayton line. As mentioned, during our stay I marched Mum there and it seemed to take ages. We didn't see a train, but, very frustratingly, we occasionally heard them from a distance and quite possibly during the long homeward trek down the dusty lanes, she in her colourful, floral print frock and me in my khaki shorts and sensible Clarks sandals.

We had made that journey to Shropshire on the Western Region's main line from Birkenhead Woodside on the route of the Paddington expresses. Above my desk - and hopefully firmly affixed - is an 11 foot carriage board in a somewhat faded chocolate brown and cream, which reads Paddington Birmingham Shrewsbury Chester Birkenhead. It is a constant reminder of the importance to us, as young trainspotters on the Wirral, of our connection to the ex-GWR system and especially to its copper-clad-chimneyed array of green namers.

We had initially planned to descend on Shrewsbury on Friday 17th February 2022, but the weather forecast was for three named gales on the trot, with consequent disruption to rail services also a possibility, and that was enough to put us off. Exactly a week later, Shrewsbury was still in the news following considerable flooding, courtesy of said storms. The TV news showed car parks under water and so we were glad we had decided to go in by train.

This week also coincided with the removal of the last legal restrictions pertaining to self-isolating with Covid. The decision has clearly been made that we are all going to have to learn to live with it from now on. Since my last trip, our family has been directly affected - and in multiple – though, thankfully, all those infected have had relatively mild symptoms. This reflects the official approach, of course, that in its current Omicron form it is more benign than its predecessors and that three jabs of vaccine should give us sufficient protection. They could have added, but didn't, that if you consider yourself to be particularly vulnerable you should assess your own personal risk in any given situation and act accordingly. On the day we finally went to Shrewsbury there were 31,933 new cases reported, 1,169 hospital admissions, 10,767 people with Covid in hospital and a further 120 deaths.

Wellington station was just how I remembered it from 1959, or perhaps I've just seen some pictures of it since - an airy layout with four tracks, including the loops that serve the main platforms. It's original buildings, dating from 1849, are thankfully still intact but not all the rooms are in regular use. A 4-car Class 158 belonging to Transport for Wales was observed heading for Birmingham. We took the 10.54 in the other direction and due into Shrewsbury at 11.07 - a Class 170 operated by West Midlands Railway. We soon passed the Wrekin on our left, which I had climbed wearing my junior school blazer, as evidenced in my mum's photo album. It shows me standing on top of the trig' point at 1,335 feet above sea level. I'd always thought it was just a bit of a hill. I wonder when I got my first anorak.

The family at the table behind us were heading for Shrewsbury on a half-term jaunt. "You say Shrewsbury", one of the children announced. "No, it's Shroesbury" chipped in another. "Shrewsbury". "Shroesbury". So, it continued almost as far as Shrewsbury, which I have always referred to as Shroesbury, but what do I know? I have enough difficulty with our own local town, Southwell. Is that South-well or Suthell? Answers on a postcard.

Shrewsbury was a spotting venue for us a number of times between 1960 and 1965, though no personal photographic evidence has survived. I'm consequently very grateful to John Dyer for allowing me to use this picture of Manor Class No. 7819 Hinton Manor in the station on 7th July 1964.

We never went round the town in the 1960s or even left the station, apart from visiting the sheds. I had completely forgotten that the station stood astride the River Severn and that there was a turreted castle next door. I was obviously somewhat blinkered in my pursuit of steam. Instead, we had wandered the central island platform moving from platform trolley to bench and back to platform trolley.

The station, itself, looked remarkably unchanged over the intervening fifty-seven years. The main buildings, now Grade II listed, the overbridge, retaining walls and the extended, shallow V-shaped metal canopies appeared to be just as they were then.

Away from the main buildings, however, the platform ends were devoid of benches, indeed completely without clutter of any kind and certainly missing were those formerly ubiquitous platform trolleys. They were substantial and unwieldy affairs, but they are central to my reminiscences of platform dwelling in the 1960s and no more so than at Shrewsbury. I recalled the part they played in our lives for an article I wrote in 2014 - one of a series for Tim Petchey's Railway Antiques Gazette. I was very grateful to Tim for giving me page space then and for giving me his blessing to draw on them once again, herein.

With a raised, metal-rimmed edge surrounding the carrying area of the trolley itself, they cut off the circulation to your lower legs quite effectively, so you had to put in quite a lot of wriggle time in the course of a whole day's trainspotting. We assumed that the unpainted and not noticeably labelled type were the railway's own property. Many were obviously the Post Office variety, painted pillar box red and with altogether smoother boards, come to think of it. Of those, some were surrounded by wire cages, so they were no use to us at all. We did not want to be enclosed like animals at the zoo. We needed to stretch out a bit more than that – and we required a more frequent feeding regime.

The trolley presented us with a seat which was often much closer to the platform end than the last official platform bench, which was always an advantage. Platform ends gave you the best chance of seeing everything that came through. If you were parked almost anywhere else on the station you could miss a loco' passing by on another track, because the view was blocked off by a train standing at your own platform.

As a case in point, John Dyer also photographed Standard Class 5 No. 73036 resting between turns on the centre road at Shrewsbury station in August 1963. She could easily have sloped off in reverse towards the sheds and in the same direction from which she had arrived, so you had to be platform end poised.

To move the trolleys any distance, you had to pull the handle down to waist height to release the brakes. At rest, the pole and handle were in the upright position and slightly inclined towards the trolley itself. Left in this position the brakes were automatically applied. Although the brakes were on, there was often some give on the wheels at the handle end, especially if it had been parked with those leading wheels a bit awry. This allowed us to sit on the trolley and rock it backwards and forwards but only for a short distance. Everybody knows how comforting rocking chairs can be and we never tired of gently swaying the things a few inches.

We were rarely disturbed by officialdom. If so, it was most likely to be a relatively polite request to "Shift", or an occasional "Come on, hop it". Being the well-mannered and easy-going youngsters we were, we would have sprung to our feet and abandoned our base, quickly stuffing loco-shed book, notebook and pen, butty box and R. White's lemonade bottle into the army surplus rucksack with the straps that never stayed tight.

Trolleys were not comfortable. You could get a splinter in your bum or on the end of your finger. Why did they always go up your finger nail? So painful! Nevertheless, we adorned them for hours, breaking our occupancy for an occasional enforced trip to the loo, or at times of particular extravagance, to the station buffet. Sometimes we would make these trips in shifts, so as not to abandon "our" trolley to other groups of trolley-covetous youths.

Finally, we vacated our lair to make for home, ready to stand in the corridor stock, taking turns with heads out of the window, risking temporary blindness and a full-frontal lobotomy in case we missed a cop passing us on the up line on our way back to Birkenhead Woodside. In this collective good cause, sweaty faces gained a gradual smattering of dust and grit from the smoke up ahead, illustrating to those at home the determined lengths we were prepared to go to in the quest for yet more numbers. Temporarily, I was off my trolley again - but we would soon be back.

From 1964, platform trolleys as we knew them

were gradually replaced by British Rail Universal Trolley Equipment (BRUTEs). These were designed without any regard for trainspotters. Caged and with a low floor, they could also travel in the brake vans. Sometimes whole trains of them would snake their way along the platform, pulled by a diminutive tractor and winding in and out of piles of suitcases and knots of passengers.

My last trainspotting trip to Shrewsbury was in December 1965. There was a profusion of Brush Type 4 diesels around and most remaining steam locos were ex-LMS and Standards. I noted Britannia Class No. 70000 Britannia as the highlight of the day. The Manor Class, that had been the great attraction at Shrewsbury and largely responsible for services on the cross-mountain route to Aberystwyth, had all gone, or rather, they were on the scrap line in the sheds – nine out of the total of thirty, in fact. Nobody in officialdom could summon the energy to kick us out this time.

The through service from Birkenhead to London only lasted until March 1967, when Ian Allan organised two special trains over the route to mark the occasion, hauled by No. 4079 Pendennis Castle and No. 7029 Clun Castle. Birkenhead Woodside closed to passengers in November of the same year and was demolished within two years. As Western Region steam ended earlier in the mid-60s than on our own London Midland Region, there was no incentive for us to go in the direction of Shrewsbury any more, as we concentrated our efforts closer to home for steam's final fling.

Shrewsbury has an interesting location, with its centre perched on a hill that is almost surrounded by a meander in the River Severn. We had hoped for a riverside walk on our recent return but that path was still largely under water. The county town has 800 listed buildings including many with that distinctive black and white Tudor-patterned, front elevation.

Charles Darwin was born in Shrewsbury and went to school there, though he was described by one of his teachers as "a very ordinary boy". His statue is outside the old school building, which is now the central library.

The blue plaque on the library wall - except that this one is black - reminds us of someone who made a lasting contribution to our understanding of where we fit into the overall scheme of things (not Judge Jeffries). I'm all in favour of blue (and other coloured) plaques. They communicate civic pride and inform us in a necessarily pithy and concise fashion. You can learn a lot about the history of a place whilst also viewing the pertinent "brick and mortar" link to the past. In an age when flagging up local attractions helps bring in tourists to aid local economies, blue plaques may be seen as a way of promoting your assets, which might even tempt a bit of exaggeration, from time to time.

Like many other places, Tenby is obviously a big believer in them to plug its historical associations. "It is said that Henry VII fled through a tunnel here on his way to France". Just a minute. "It is said that..?" Since when has "It is said that.." been a justification for a blue plaque? Who said it, anyway, the bloke in the pub down the road? I had thought blue plaques were statements of fact about who had actually lived in a particular house and that they usually went on to tell you exactly when, as well. This dented my belief in blue plaques a bit, especially on this particular town trail. What next, I thought, "They do say in these parts...ooh, argh" or "Some folks do think, 'appen, 'appen...".

Blue plaque number two in Tenby, at East Rock House, claims it as a fact, but our accompanying town trail gives the game away again. "In 1802 Sir William and Lady Hamilton....may well have stayed at this family house". "May well? Oh, yes, are you sure?" By the time we had passed the pub where Dylan Thomas "..was said to have" got so drunk that he left behind the manuscript for Under Milk Wood, and an advert for a local restaurant that was getting in on the act by claiming to produce "the best pizzas in the world", we had just about suspended belief in signage of all description.

Many informative black and white cast-iron signs

preceded the blue plaque phenomenon, of course, but they still had the capacity to go a bit over the top on occasions. The inhabitants of early nineteenth century Ramsgate, for example, were so impressed with a royal visitor that the harbour-side inscription reads, "To George IV, the King Of Great Britain and Ireland, the inhabitants and visitors of Ramsgate and the directors and trustees of the harbour have erected this obelisk as a grateful reminder of His Majesty's gracious condescension in selecting this port for his embarkation of the 25th September in progress to his Kingdom of Hannover and His happy Return on the 8 November 1821". He only passed through, got on a boat and came back. End of. I mean, come on.

The inside of Shrewsbury's library was welcoming enough – a modern well-equipped interior to add to a handsome historic exterior. Chris picked up her customary paperwork from the tourist information section and Sandra enquired about an eatery that I'd noticed when browsing through the internet's What's on in Shrewsbury? website. I have always liked libraries since I adopted a female librarian who was in her late twenties when I was aged about 11, making daily visits to see her on my way home from school and taking away everything that I could find by Enid Blyton, Richmal Crompton, Anthony Buckeridge, Frank Richards and Conan Doyle, and probably in that order.

The last time we were in Liverpool, we visited the newly refurbished Central Library, one of a line of three imposing Victorian public buildings in the William Brown Street Conservation Area, sitting opposite the equally magnificent St George's Hall, just below Lime Street station. They have made a fine job of it, keeping all the best bits, like the circular Picton reading room, whilst opening out the central space inside the main entrance with a series of mezzanine levels joined by prominent stairways, all culminating in a dramatic glass dome and with roof access providing views over the city.

I gravitated towards the local history section, where I found a multitude of books about Merseyside that I did not know existed, many of them self-published efforts, like my own. I find it refreshing that stock buyers take a punt on self-published books. Some library services won't go near them with a barge-pole, fearing schoolboy errors and amateurish presentation. They sometimes have a point. Authors of books aimed at niche markets can't necessarily afford the services of professional publishers, proof readers or literary agents. Unless they have been extremely careful, therefore, they lay themselves open to inevitable criticism. It is the easiest thing in the world to overlook a basic error, however many times you read the proof. Although I'm tempted to trawl through such books for their cock-ups, I'm actually very pleased they are there. They give voice to those who would otherwise remain unheard, yet the stories and observations that they contain are brimming with experience, insight, closely observed familiarity and - in this case, certainly - an abundant affection for their city. They are rough diamonds granted the opportunity to rub shoulders with literary masterpieces. Their inclusion in such a prestigious location takes foresight from the decision makers. It does not surprise me at all that in Liverpool they are given full rein.

We did not stay long enough in Shrewsbury library on this occasion to investigate their policy towards self-publishers, but we did find out where our proposed destination for lunch was. The River View Café is located at The Parade shops, which occupy the stylish and beautifully preserved Grade II listed building completed in 1830 as the Royal Salop Infirmary. The winter sun granted us just enough warmth to sit out on the terrace with panoramic views across the still swollen and fast-moving river below.

I could pick out Severn Bridge Junction signalbox, itself Grade II listed and recently renovated. It is the largest operational mechanical signalbox in the world, a status it is expected to maintain for some time to come, as signalling through Shrewsbury remains a mixture of semaphore and colour light. The recent and tastefully designed riverside development in the foreground appeared to have taken the signalbox into account, to present a noticeably harmonious overall view.

We wandered off towards the river and found a remarkably cheery gentleman (given the circumstances) pumping water out of his cellar whilst sweeping up in his hallway. He was resigned to this as an increasingly regular occurrence, though his demeanour may have been a little different had this not been a second home that he rents out – when it's not under water, that is.

The Shrewsbury Museum and Art Gallery was featuring a display of the work of Ladybird book artists. I recognised some of the names, including Rowland Hiller, Ronald Lampitt and Septimus Scott, because they had also been railway poster and carriage print artists in that same mid-twentieth century era. Ian reminded me that a copy of Scott's stunning Art Deco quad royal poster, showing a bathing beauty sitting on the top diving board at New Brighton's former (and also Art Deco) outdoor pool, is on display at the entrance to the Station Hall at the NRM.

Back at Shrewsbury station, we said our goodbyes to our friends and waited for our train. It was a busy scene and the train announcement loudspeaker system was in overdrive. If we were using a Transport for Wales service face masks were still compulsory. Buses were still replacing trains on the Aberystwyth line, due to a "problem currently under investigation", as the message had gone out rather mysteriously on our arrival, earlier in the day. That turned out to be due to flood water problems, too.

I drifted off. "The train now standing at platform one is the 8.55 for London Paddington, calling at Chester General, Wrexham General, Ruabon, Gobowen, Shrewsbury, Wellington, Wolverhampton Low Level, Birmingham Snow Hill......" When I close my eyes and whisk myself back, I can still hear it now, booming out and echoing around under Birkenhead Woodside station's overall roof. Similar routines were repeated at the start of our journeys from Liverpool Central High Level, Lime Street and Exchange. Sometimes suddenly crackling into life with a "ping" when switched on; sometimes coming across a little intermittently when the microphone was not properly connected. Sometimes the whole performance was accompanied by background hiss; sometimes you could hear other people's conversations in the background. It was fallible human beings wrestling with intermediate technology. It was perfectly imperfect, to me.

How it has changed. At the larger stations, at least, the received pronunciation of the main line termini and the regional accents of the provinces are largely gone. In their place is a staccato, characterless and clearly computerised, electronic system, which is not just detached from reality but composed of individual words and phrases that sound like they have been uttered by a number of sanitised, straight-jacketed, corporate individuals, rearranged and then finally delivered by a robot. It is devoid of personality. Its automated output is so distant and functional that it smacks of disregard and even of rudeness - another example of how human interaction has become less valued than technology.

My own favourite "old school" - and as far as I can recall, very polite, though very regional - public address system message came on a Peter Handford, Argo Transacord extended play vinyl record, which turned at forty-five revolutions per minute on my Dansette record player's turntable, on those occasions that keeping the beat was allowed to take a breather. It came with an auto-changer that allowed us to stack records in multiple. Now that did seem pretty high-tech' to us. It was called Change at Templecombe. The EP looked like a seven-inch diameter "single", but it had two or three tracks squeezed onto each side. I had five such discs. It was EAF125 that gave me so much pleasure for years after I had made my own two summer holiday pilgrimages to Templecombe in 1964 and 1965.

Bear with me, because I don't think I have heard the actual recording for forty odd years and so this is from memory. It was preceded by a loud click as the PA was switched on. "Templecombe, Templecombe. This is Templecombe. Change trains here for Bath and Bournemouth lines. Over the bridge to number three platform for trains to Bath and Bournemouth. The train at platform one is for Exeter Central, calling at Sherborne, Yeovil Junction, Crewkerne, Axminster, Seaton Junction, Honiton, Sidmouth Junction, Whimple and Exeter Central. Change at Exeter Central for Exeter St David's.........."

If the station announcements have changed beyond recognition, they have certainly thought up a whole load more stuff to tell us about. How did we ever get by without falling down the gap? There is absolutely no chance of us leaving any luggage unattended for as much as a split second. We are frequently reminded that our every move is being watched because "CCTV is in operation at this station" and that we should report anything that looks suspicious. On the trains themselves, there is also a barrage of information and that is in addition to the digital VDU displays, but at least it is usually someone actually speaking. I'm very happy with that. I would much prefer to listen to a real human with a local accent, that marvellous phenomenon that divides us and unites us as a nation, all at the same time. I sometimes hear a bit of sniggering from along the coach when a distinctly regional passenger manager is on the air. I can do without that sort of contempt, to be honest.

In the age of the fixed telephone, trackside telephone wires and telegraph poles also came as standard. It was mesmerising to look out of the carriage window as the lines repeatedly rose and fell between the post tops – predictable, benign waves reaching the top of a beach then receding. I always look out of the train window. I can't concentrate on a book. Who knows what is about to turn up outside the window? I might miss something. In America, travelling by train over thousands of miles from coast to coast, a total of two coyotes were spotted. I missed them both because I had gone to the toilet at the wrong moment. Luckily, though, I was there for the sole bald eagle which showed itself in a leafless tree near the Colorado River.

I snapped back into the present as the train for Wellington pulled in. I sat back and contemplated our return to Shrewsbury. In 1831, Charles Darwin had boarded a horse-drawn coach outside the Lion Hotel, Shrewsbury's leading coaching inn, and headed off to join the Beagle. Over the next five years, he collected the animal, plant and fossil samples from four continents that would lead to his theory of natural selection of 1859. According to his son, Francis, when Charles Darwin revisited Shrewsbury with his daughter in 1869, he had communicated to her a strong impression of his love for his old home town. Love of place again, and I share that affection for my own home town of Wallasey. In Darwin's case, it might have had very little to do with the coming of the railways while he was away. The trains had already been running into Shrewsbury for over twenty years by the time he returned. At least, that would have made his journey back home a speedier and more comfortable affair than his earlier departure was likely to have been.

11. Nuneaton

After my first ever visit to Nuneaton - on my birthday in 2015 - I wrote up the details and included them in the railway heritage blog that I set up in the following year and which contains over 750 posts at the time of writing. The increasing cost of rail travel was much in the news at that time, so - quite literally - no change there then....

Much is written about the rising cost of travelling by train and I know that for commuters the outlay can be horrendous. My guess is that the rewards elsewhere for jumping on board each morning justify the outlay in most cases. As the railways are more popular than ever, it is hard to see how cheaper tickets for regular users at busy times is ever going to happen. I can think of some other campaigning groups in society who might be more deserving of my support. If you are flexible in your travel plans, book in advance and travel at cheaper times, train travel need not be a particularly expensive business at all, and it's even cheaper with a rail card.

It has become a bit of a pattern that I celebrate my birthday with a trip on the trains, and so it was again this year, with an East Midlands Trains Day Ranger ticket, chosen destination - Nuneaton. Cheaper than the equivalent day return and very good value for my day out it seemed to me, even though I could have travelled a great deal further and on many more trains, if either hours or miles had been the main aim of the venture.

I see that the Green Party is advocating the re-nationalisation of the railways as part of its 2015 General Election manifesto. An online campaign on the same tack comes my way periodically. I'm not so sure. At the time, I was opposed to the sell-off of the utility companies and our most important national assets, especially as the shares were often undervalued and effectively made the well-off even richer, without necessarily ensuring the best deal for the taxpayer, thereafter. Most European countries recognise the value of holding on to a national rail system. Perhaps I will have a clearer idea of where I stand after my day out.

At Fiskerton station I am met by a rash of notices all saying the same thing. "Safety Notice. Pedestrian gates at this station will now be closed and secured for the passage of trains. The gates will only be opened when the train has passed and only by Network Rail staff. Please allow time to catch your train". Oh dear, I think there must have been an incident. The 10.04 to Leicester, a 2-car Class 156 unit, is busy and I now know that I have walked to the wrong end. As I sit down there is a very pervasive smell of sweaty feet. It is almost overpowering, but this is the only area that has vacant seats and now I know why. I survey my fellow passengers for visible signs of less than rigorous personal hygiene. I decide on a middle-aged man with metal studs around his mouth and very greasy hair and when he gets out at Nottingham the odour goes with him, but there again, so do 90% of the other passengers. I have no proof that his socks are not spotless. I know I may be guilty of a bit of stereotyping here and I will never know if my hunch is right. I wonder where the smell is going next, but only for a second.

It is obviously going to be a day of new notices. The one in the toilet says, "Please don't flush nappies, sanitary towels, paper towels, gum, old phones, unpaid bills, junk mail, your ex's sweater, hopes, dreams or goldfish down this toilet". I do as I am told, but I appreciate the attempt at a humorous approach to what is clearly a real problem. Our chatty conductor guard opens the doors at Syston. "My God, where has everyone come from?", is his greeting to those approaching the train. "You can tell its half term", he concludes. He has already told me he has renewed his house insurance twice over by mistake, and he has bought himself a conservatory on eBay. We have only been friends for five minutes. "Going to Nuneaton are you?..... Are you sure?", he quips. On our approach to Leicester, we pass a row of forlorn Class 56s. They are in such poor external condition that I can only presume that they are on their way to being scrapped. They look like they have already given up the fight for their own survival. I realise that I still think of the Class 56 as being one of the more recent diesel types, so that suddenly seems like a quick lifetime for a locomotive and quite a chunk out of mine, too. Leicester station is a hive of activity. The public address system is having a field day. I am requested to tell a policeman if I am suspicious of anything, roughly the same advice my mum gave me about 60 years ago, so it must be right. I tried that once, when I was about eleven. I had been threatened by another boy who would not let me go past him on my bike. It just so happened that there was a policeman standing nearby on traffic duty. He completely ignored my request for assistance and carried on waving at cars, simultaneously denting my faith in the constabulary for some time to come.

My next train is a 2-car Turbostar Class 170, which is obviously a great name for a space rocket as well as a train. It is on its way to Birmingham and it is packed. Like the Class 156 before it, the décor is attractive and it is comfortable, smooth and very nippy.

I am getting quite peckish by the time I get to Nuneaton, so, as always, lunch becomes the priority. Unfortunately, it is raining steadily and I'm not exactly sure how far I would have to walk to enjoy the delights of the town centre. The guard has hardly gone out of his way to sell it to me. I opt for the buffet on the station, although I don't recognise the name of the franchise and it definitely isn't part of the chain that my wife would recommend as providing the best coffee of all. I settle for a poor cup of coffee that she would have certainly left standing there and one of the blandest sandwiches I have ever tasted. Produced by a nationally known company, it must have decided its sandwich making policy on the grounds of upsetting the smallest amount of people with a determination never to offend taste buds by running anything past them that they might be able to give a score to. Actually, I don't think my taste buds were employed at all. They were superfluous to the exercise. My snack is partly rescued by a packet of crisps which tries gamely to help my sandwich over the line. On the side of the packet it says, "Can you help an older person get out more?" Well, in a way, they just have. "Too many older people are stuck at home, day after lonely day". Not yet, mate, I thought. So says the one who treats himself to a ride on a train once a year on his birthday. Well at least I'm here – in Nuneaton. I know how to live.

I had chosen Nuneaton for what I imagined was a very good reason. It is on the West Coast Main Line. I live near the East Coast Main Line. I thought I would see what was happening over the other side, as it were. I walk up platform one, passing the location of what I guess was once an acceptable buffet. The rain drips through the holes in the roof. The feral pigeons are staying put somewhere up there, too, as the spattering of droppings below their roost testifies. They've probably had their fill of discarded sandwich remains, if they think they are worth bothering with at all, that is.

The trains are excellent. Between platforms 3 and 4, the Pendolinos shoot through at, I was told, 125 mph, a little faster than the Voyagers at 120. You really do have to stand well back from the edge. The yellow line is there for a reason. As the Pendolinos approach, there is a noticeable spray from the contact between their leading wheels and the wet track. Momentarily, it reminds me of steam from the cylinders of the Coronation Pacifics that took the same road in times past, but that is just wishful thinking. Where there is contact with the overhead wire, the rain shoots off the pantograph in a fountain, too, all adding to an overall effect of grace and speed. It is actually a very impressive sight.

Nuneaton has two newer platforms, numbers 6 and 7, furthest from the entrance and on the east side of the station. These are used by the Cross Country services between Birmingham and Stansted Airport, which I have sampled to get here.

I notice that I am not alone. There are other spotters here. I even see a young lad in a bobble hat, just like the one I had worn on Crewe station in 1963. The notes he is making in his notebook are meticulous and more detailed than anything I would ever have considered necessary. Another youngster is filming the action with a tiny camera sitting aloft a full-size tripod. My generation is well represented as well.

As I am spotting the spotters, I am interrupted by a middle-aged lady in a long flowing skirt who looks a bit the worse for wear. She has an unintelligible question for me about the timetable she is pointing at. I mime ignorance and shrug my shoulders, which luckily does the trick as she turns away to see if anyone else is listening. There is a group of men of a certain age at the south end of platform one. These are the regulars, I tell myself. The two enthroned on fold-up camping chairs are holding court. There is another group on numbers 4 and 5, sitting on and standing around a bench, eating chips out of paper.

The freight trains keep on coming. It is great to see that side of the railways is so busy. Classes 37, 66, 70, 90 and even a 92 are represented. The container trains are pretty full and there are car carriers and ballast trains in the mix. I strike up a conversation with a bloke who is on his own, like me. He has come up from Rugby because he knows that a landslip near Coventry had led to the diversion of even more freight trains through Nuneaton than usual. He found this out on Realtime Trains, he tells me. "You have to use the advanced search". Not for the first time in my life, I feel totally inadequate over a technology issue, but I resolve to get up to speed - well, as soon as I've got myself a mobile phone, anyway.

The water continues to pour through the holes in the roof, but the spotters are undeterred. My new mate says that he has noticed that another group of them are holed up in a waiting room in the middle of the station. He does not associate with them because he thinks they can be a little intimidating to members of the travelling public, swearing and talking loudly and obsessively in a way that others might find uncomfortable and off-putting, as though they had stumbled in on a private party that just goes on forever.

As we chat, we are interrupted by a man wielding an umbrella. He talks passionately about five or six random issues that are much on his mind without stopping to draw breath. He then promises that when he returns from the toilet, he will tell us exactly why his shoes are so dirty. They are extremely muddy, but as he has not come back, we are denied access to the mucky shoe story. Perhaps he is saving that one for someone else.

I say goodbye to my interesting and knowledgeable recent acquaintance, a truly modern spotter, with his finger on the pulse. I take off again on the Turbostar to Leicester, passing that station's First Class Lounge on the way in. I settle for the Pumpkin coffee bar instead and sit by the radiator. I reflect on my lack of gadgetry. Everyone in here has got something to listen to or some piece of equipment or other to fiddle with. I notice that head-sets, which started off large and then went small, are now large again. There is probably a good reason for that. The train home from Leicester is now a busy commuter train, as well as carrying families back home after their half term city treat. The HST engineers' train, the Derby-based flying banana, passes us going south at Trent Junction.

I have learnt quite a lot from my day out. Trainspotting is alive and well and prospering in Nuneaton. In my admittedly small sample, the trains are clean, warm and reliable. They run to time, and the information about them, both visual and audible, is plentiful. The railways are buzzing. There is an enormous variety of liveries for locomotives and rolling stock. The trains are very well used. The staff are generally helpful and friendly. Freight is definitely on the move – surely more so than in immediately preceding decades, away from the coalfields, at least? It gives every appearance of being a system that is working well. The question at the back of my mind is how would re-nationalisation help at this moment and exactly who would it help? In years gone by I was firmly opposed to the break-up of British Rail. Now I look at all this and I'm not so sure that I can see how taking it back into public ownership at this stage would bring significant advantages. If it is a reduction in ticket prices that is at the back of the campaign, then where would the money come from instead for new stock? Surely, it's better that those who use the system most frequently pay most for its gradual improvement and it gives every sign of being gradually improved to me.

On a personal note, a world of high tech' trainspotting is there for the taking, but I will definitely have to upgrade my IT skills. In the past, that has meant responding to a specific need appropriately, so, for example, I got to grips with the word processing challenge because I wanted to write stuff. Now the bar has been raised and the next one is facing me head on in the form of an iPhone and Realtime Trains. Maybe I'll go for it.

I made it safely home on 19 February 2015, and embarked on certain changes of habit soon afterwards. I acquired a mobile phone – a pass-me-down from my daughter, who likes to keep a bit more up to date with things than I do. That phone, itself now ageing, informs me that it will no longer let me contact my friends on WhatsApp after this month, so I now have to acquire another one to replace it. I did get into Realtime Trains and have found it very useful indeed. We also now have some decent camera equipment to use, which I'm gradually learning how to make best use of, whereas I had not taken any pictures at Nuneaton in 2015. I have also reconsidered my views about the re-nationalisation of the railways. At the moment, I would say that I'm in favour of it, because I don't see why a natural monopoly can really benefit from the sort of competition that makes capitalism work in other more obvious settings where there is a realistic choice for consumers, and because I don't see that it is fair that shareholders should gain from what should be a public service run for those who use it, and who should therefore be its real beneficiaries. That is actually very galling. However, ask me in a few years and I may have changed my mind again. That is why I'm not a politician. I listen to the arguments and I change my mind sometimes. As a former colleague once informed me, I am no more than a broken reed. When I finished work, another colleague contradicted him by describing me as a highly principled professional, but he didn't know me very well.

I realise now how out of touch I had become with the railway scene in general by 2015. After retirement, I had resolved to find more time for my old hobby again. I was stepping back into an arena that I thought I knew, but I soon realised that I was seriously off the pace. This has been amplified further since getting back on track again during late 2021 and early 2022, especially when tab-hanging on the platforms to these clued-up and committed youngsters that "the railway fancy", as it has been described by the railway social historian, Ian Carter, just keeps on attracting. I find this quite heart-warming. I will now make a lunch time appointment with Chris, so that she can help me set up my new phone in time for my imminent return to Nuneaton. I also have to admit to my previous ignorance about the diesel facility next to the Midland Main Line north of Leicester station. UK Rail Leasing clearly provides a very useful service overhauling locomotives and putting them back to work.

The UK Health Security Agency stopped publishing dashboard updates for weekends on the Government's Coronavirus data website from the 21st February 2022. This would appear to be part of an official relaxation in the overall messaging that adds to the impression that the worst is firmly now behind us. Covid no longer features in the main BBC News programmes as a matter of course, which it did, daily, for two years. The Government website no longer highlights daily infection totals, showing instead new infection totals over the previous 7 days. All the regular indicators of infection levels continue to move in the right direction. Station public address systems on my latest trip did not mention masks, nor did I see any written notices about them. Certainly, very few of us wore them whilst on board the trains.

On Thursday 3rd March 2022, I drove to Hinckley station in Leicestershire, a journey over just over an hour from home. My off-peak ticket in the station car park takes me from 10.00 on the dot until 2.30 on Friday morning, should I wish to see it out. That left me wondering how three o'clock in the morning could be interpreted as peak time travel. From Hinckley, which I discovered during entry is the home of Triumph motor bikes, it is just six minutes to Nuneaton on the 10.06. The Class 170 has come from Leicester and is heading for Birmingham New Street. The return journey ticket with my senior railcard costs £4.25. I look for a table in my section with a full complement of four empty seats, but the one I had my eye on turns out to have a man with his back to me and his dog. The dog is on a lead, but I still have to circumnavigate his rear end that is protruding into the passageway, as I take the next seat down the carriage. Nevertheless, this brown curly-haired example seems quite benign and I'm only going to be there for a few minutes. My mum had let us have a cat when we were kids and so we have had one ever since until last year (a series of replacements rather than the same one, obviously). My daughter brought home the last one immediately after we had declared, "That's it. No more pets". She promptly left home and failed to take the cat with her. He proceeded to stick it out with us for the next 16 years. Consequently, I see myself as a cat person rather than a dog person. I've always been a bit wary of dogs, probably through lack of familiarity. They used to burst our plastic footballs in the park from time to time, when they weren't crapping on the pitch so that we got soiled jeans and trainers to take home, removing our footwear in the vestibule so they didn't stink the house out or spoil the carpet. That was in spite of the park in question having a designated "dog run" section. Those dogs just didn't read the signs. We used to joke about that special aroma of "wet dog" perfume. I find dogs often unpredictable, sometimes intrusive and occasionally downright scary. Their frequent barking from a nearby garden disturbs the peace when I'm sitting outside on an otherwise pleasant summer afternoon. None of our group of friends grew up with dogs at home. If we had, I'm sure that my perspective would be different.

For one of my big birthdays, we went to Nice on the Eurostar and the TGV, crossing Paris with a few minutes available to admire the amazing Train Bleu restaurant at Gare de Lyon. The French are big cat and dog lovers, too, it seems. Both in Paris and in the coastal resorts, I noticed a penchant, especially amongst ladies of a certain age, for both cats and tiny dogs on leads, in baskets – even of the cycle handlebar attachment type, or simply tucked under one arm. They are clearly considered to be a fashion accessory.

Taking the busy early morning return TGV to Paris, and in plenty of time to take our two reserved seats in the direction of travel and at a table, an elderly but very French lady with a diminutive dog strode past us along the platform, obviously looking for her own seat. "She's going to sit here with that dog', I said to Chris, and she did, taking her place opposite us.

Never mind, I thought, it's only a few hundred miles of close-up dog. The dog spent Nice to Avignon sniffing my ankles. I turned to Chris. "It's doing heavy breathing on my leg". From Avignon to Lyon, it slept on the seat next to its owner. "About time", I said, from behind my hands. From Lyon to Paris, it sat in its basket a few inches from my face, as I ate my previously purchased cheese and ham baguette. "Don't you dare", I muttered in its general direction.

"At least it doesn't stink", I munched sideways to Chris as the dog watched me eat every mouthful. "Why has it got that stupid bow round its neck?", I added. Chris looked up from her book and shrugged her shoulders.
Approaching Gare de Lyon, my attention drawn by a sudden rash of graffiti on every available concrete surface - of which there are plenty - as well as on the flanks of the parked-up suburban commuter stock, people suddenly and somewhat feverishly began to gather their possessions together, as though there was only going to be a two-minute stop at the

terminus station. "Can you reach my coat on the luggage rack, please?" asked the French lady with perfect English who was sitting opposite us. The dog looked at me smugly. I'm sure he mouthed, "Boom-boom".

In the days before discarded face masks and surgical gloves became the second-most frequently viewed litter on grass verges and footpaths to fast food wrappers and paper cups, little blue, black and even pink-coloured bags of dog poo had become quite a thing. Some were hung on trees like Christmas decorations. One bright, warm summer evening, we sat at a picnic table outside the pub and looked out over the River Trent. The swallows wheeled and swooped. A lady plonked her bag of dog poo down on the next table. "Where's the bin?", she said, but it was too late. My cheese and onion crisps had already lost their flavour. I know I can only lose friends by having a go at dogs. I'm not. I'm having a pop at a few dog owners.

Which reminds me. Another special place for me is Dawlish in Devon and especially Brunel's GWR sea wall. At a time when bringing up three small children and entertaining them during the summer holidays was paramount, we spent weeks away in Teignmouth and Dawlish, where I could build cars made of sand on the beach, scour rock pools for starfish and watch the action on the main line at the same time. I'm thus drawn back to Dawlish periodically to indulge myself in happy holiday reminiscences.

On one such occasion in more recent times, we had gone back there to watch a steam special from Bristol that was heading for Kingswear. Class A4 No. 60009 Union of South Africa performed that duty one sunny day in the late summer of 2018.

While I waited, camera in hand, Chris, being a more adventurous soul, went for a wander along the breakwater. I turned back towards the railway. A yappy dog ran straight at me, stopping just short - but still very agitated. This sometimes happens when we are walking or cycling on the trail at home. The dog owners' default position is always, "He's OK, he's only being friendly". Every time when this has happened previously, I've murmured something polite, smiled and moved on without a fuss, even if I have already been slobbered on, had my crotch sniffed or received dirty paw marks on my trousers.

This time, for reasons unknown, I did not raise my head, I did not smile, I simply covered my groin with both hands - as if defending a free kick in the wall on the edge of the penalty area. Then I walked on. This was interpreted as an affront. "Do 'im, Berts", came the response. At this point I did look round but both the owner and the man he was talking to made a point of looking away. It was as though the command had mysteriously drifted down from above. I know how important dogs are to some folk. I understand the special bond that many people have with them, but not everyone feels as comfortable in the company of dogs as some dog owners imagine and that is what I would like some dog owners to consider. I left my seat as we approached Nuneaton and asked the dog's owner what sort he was. "Cockapoo", he replied. "I thought he was", I answered, "My daughter and family have just got one as a puppy". So, now, I'm just going to have to get used to it, though I am since informed that the new arrival is actually a cavapoo, so I'm learning all the time. I'm sure we'll get on fine, eventually.

So, what's changed during the seven years since I last set foot on Nuneaton station? The first thing is that it is now cloudy after a bright start but at least it's not pouring down like last time. I make for the station buffet again. It has changed hands in the interim (no surprise there) and in an unplanned déjà vu moment I settle for a packet of crisps to accompany my sandwich brought from home. It costs a whopping £1.60 - mind you it is of "grab bag" size, though it still only weighs 34 grams. The spotters are here again. My initial survey finds 16 but this rises to over 20, including just one under the age of sixty, at a guess, and he has a large tripod with an even tinier camera mounted on the top – maybe the same guy as on my previous visit. I settle down on my platform end bench for lunch, while the formerly Virgin and now (since 2019) Avanti West Coast Trains Pendolinos sail through regularly and at speed, interspersed with Class 66s on container freights, the cross-country passenger services and the electric multiple units that augment the longer distance expresses on the West Coast Main Line.

The modern station benches are not in any labelled railway house style. They are lightly varnished wooden slats on a sturdy green metal base. I have to settle for one without a back support, as all the others are taken by small groups of enthusiasts, as always, deep in conversation about their common purpose. West Midlands Trains, who run the station, have made a bit of an effort with the provision of some recently added flower displays, including one in which new shoots are already rising this early in the spring from an old travel trunk with an open lid and the sides adorned with some random travel stickers. Though it shows positive intent, it may take a bit of developing to qualify for the Chelsea Flower Show any time soon. The LNR aluminium lettering on the side of the trolley presumably stands for local nature reserve.

Nuneaton station was built for the London North Western Railway and opened in 1847. As the rail network developed the station buildings were replaced in stages. The current frontage and clock tower date from 1915. Known as

Nuneaton Trent Valley until 1969, it is a marked improvement on Tamworth. Birmingham to Leicester services have used the flyover to the north of the station since 2004, and a 2012 chord to the west of it enables traffic from Felixtowe going north to join the WCML without impeding other traffic on the main line. Inspection of the facilities complete, I was still listening intently to a recorded message that had been broadcast regularly over the PA system ever since I had arrived. "As a result of a recent policy change, we no longer accept _____on any of our trains or stations". What could it be? I was genuinely perplexed and I couldn't quite make it out. Surely not trainspotters? I'd seen a notice banning smoking, vaping and e-cigarettes. It wasn't that either but it gave me the clue I needed. It was e-scooters. The change in policy is obviously working. I wasn't bothered by any of them all day. Just to finally wrap up the dog business, on the day I put the finishing touches to this section, I was confronted by a very angry pooch whilst cycling my bike on the trail - a former railway line near to home which is now a multi-use recreational path. He ran straight at me and I was forced to stop. I'd already announced my presence to his minder with an inoffensive little "ping" on my bell. The owner made no effort to rein him in verbally. "Dogs come first", was, I think, a relatively jovial attempt by him at an icebreaker. "He's got a real thing about bicycles at the moment". I slowly moved off but the dog stuck to his task, barking and jumping around alongside me and still within ankle nipping range. "Be better off on a lead", I suggested, but no response was forthcoming. Surely, people come first, I thought, as I finally escaped. I always come up with my better lines when the moment has already passed.

12. Crewe

I'd already been to Crewe for the day on thirteen previous occasions by the time I began to document things a bit more thoroughly in the summer of 1962. That showed a certain commitment to the cause, I would suggest. As a schoolboy with limited personal income from a paper round and a short-lived spell selling Wall's ice cream from a hand-pushed cart round a Birkenhead housing estate on Sundays, I still largely relied for money for travel tickets on my generous but not wealthy parents. I know how lucky I was.

At certain times throughout my life, perhaps when I have felt particularly under pressure for one reason or another, I have craved a little innocent escapism. On such occasions, when I have shut my eyes and dreamt the daydream of my choice, it could easily have gone something like this....

Is there anywhere I would like to be transported back to more than Crewe in the early 1960s? Was there a more important place name in the world for me when I was thirteen than Crewe? Then, Crewe was the centre of the universe. It was far enough away from home to feel you were going somewhere special but near enough for a comfortably timed day trip by train. We didn't have to get up ridiculously early to get there and we even had an interesting choice of routes to choose from in order to reach it.

Sometimes we go from New Brighton to Liverpool Central and walk up to Lime Street. We could actually get there by a slower and more circuitous route via Birkenhead Park, Bidston and a walk between Chester Northgate and

General, just for a change, but we never do. Our favourite is to start off on the number ten bus to Birkenhead Hamilton Square from Stroude's corner in Wallasey. The joint service is provided alternately between the two boroughs by yellow Wallasey Corporation examples and blue ones from Birkenhead.

After a short walk down to Woodside station, a Fairburn tank whisks us to Chester on the Paddington expresses, hammering along the four-track sections between Rock Ferry and Hooton and then on through Capenhurst. No. 42236 pulls up in the bay platforms serving the ex-GWR lines out of Chester. It is detached from the train and waits for its rostered return to Birkenhead later on in the day. County Class No. 1025 County of Radnor is attached at the other end to take it on towards Birmingham Snow Hill.

If there is time before the next train to Crewe, we grab a mug of tea at the buffet next to the main station entrance and then it is over the footbridge in time for Stanier Black Five No. 45426 coming off the North Wales line to take us on. First it is Chester sheds on the left as we pick up speed, so we have to be alert, as always. Past Beeston Castle and we are slowing for Crewe in no time. The Works is on the left and if you stand on tiptoe in the corridor with your head out of the window there is just a chance of being able to read the smokebox number plates on the condemned un-rebuilt Patriots on the other side of the wall. There is just one long siding here alongside the workshop buildings.

There is no time to lose. It is straight over to the other side of the coach, as we round the curve and the station comes into view. What a splendid sight 5A Crewe North sheds is, just teeming with red and green engines in addition to the usual black ones. We start shouting out the numbers and the resulting scrawlings in the note book are off the ruled lines in no time. Talk about pressure. At the back of our minds, we actually know that this is probably an unnecessary panic as we have it in mind to bunk 5A as a matter of course later in the day, but you never know. It is not a good idea to count our chickens too early on. Brief arguments ensue over the misreading of a grubby cab side number, an issue we can't immediately resolve as the locomotive in question has already disappeared behind something else. In the end, we go with the majority, or maybe it is just the loudest voice.

Coronation Class No. 46228 Duchess of Rutland shimmers in the sunlight, primed for the north, all fizz and pent-up energy. I get butterflies in my tummy as I anticipate a successful hit on Crewe North, eager to see what is lurking in the depths of the shed, on parade at the mouth of the half roundhouse, or being prepared in the yard and currently out of sight. Crewe North is not that easy. Past the little single-storey general store at the end of the road bridge, the one that sells the Ian Allan abc books, and then we take a right into the warren of Victorian terraces. We know the way to the main entrance so well, but we are assured of nothing. We pass other groups of lads on their way back but we don't quiz them, because this is our own mission. It is always a busy route and at the entrance itself we have to go down a narrow passageway adjacent to the offices. There are windows in the offices and the foreman can see who is going past, but only if he is on the lookout. Rather than crouch down and look stupidly furtive, we prefer a short, sharp walking pace without looking sideways and then just hope for the best. With a bit of luck, the foreman is deep in conversation. If we can get past that bit without being challenged, we could be OK, as it then opens out into the main shed. Our plan is that if we are ever stopped, we would always ask politely if we could have a look round, knowing that the answer would be a scornful "No" (or worse) but probably acting sensibly enough to take the sting out of the situation, as we turn on our heels in unison and make for the exit.

Right at the last, we pass a forlorn group of lads coming the other way. "Got kicked out", they tell us. "He's standing outside his office". We get cold feet because we know we are next in the firing line. All is not lost. We know another way in and so another few minutes is taken up as we walk round through yet more streets until we are on the other side of the shed. Here there is a high wire fence adjacent to more sturdy railings, which separate us from the shed yard and the coaling plant. The flimsy fencing is frequently being attacked and then patched up again. Sometimes there is a small gap in the railings. On other occasions lads have burrowed like badgers in the dirt at the foot of the fence and then tried to curl up the wire at the base. We grovel in the cinders and we get in. Hearts are pounding now. We look around and leg it towards the first line of engines that offers some cover, as well as a host of new numbers. We work our way systematically round the site, finishing at the main entrance before walking steadily but warily past the offices and out into the daylight. Only then does the exhilaration hit us. We are ecstatic. We talk about the new cops that we know we have made without looking them up, edging towards the classing of the Semis, or taking us within one of finishing off the Prinnies, before they are all withdrawn.

From there, Gresty Lane sheds seems like miles away, but we go for it anyway, and probably at a canter. It is only two-road but it has Westerns, usually Halls or even Granges. It is in the shadow of the Mornflake Oats breakfast cereal factory. It is a tiring trek on a hot day, but it just has to be done. South sheds, 5B, is usually fairly full, but lacks the namers that are so plentiful at North, though it could still turn up the odd Jubilee or Britannia. On the way we have to pass the new diesel depot with a handful of English Electric Type 4's humming away outside. This is a difficult nut to crack and we barely give it the time of day, but we do write down the numbers we can see from the path. South is a sprawling site and you have to cross many railway tracks on walkways to reach it. It feels a little open and we are really a bit vulnerable, both to being spotted and ejected and with having to keep an eye on moving traffic. I don't ever remember being asked to leave from here, and at both big sheds there are always other groups of lads milling around.

Without permits as part of an official school party, we are usually stumped for access to the Works, though on this occasion we manage to tag along with another organised group and we are delighted to have "beaten the system" this once. Sometimes the crocodiles of lads and their leaders queuing at the works entrance are enormous. A couple of elderly works employees in uniform with shiny flat hats are assigned to take us round, one at the front and one at the rear. The Works is massive and full of surprises – locos from other parts that we weren't expecting to see and new diesels under construction. The old hands don't look up from their tasks but some of the young blades take the Mickey or just smirk at us in a derisory fashion.

Back at the station, we are just in time for the arrival of the afternoon express from Glasgow to Birmingham, which is usually hauled by a Coronation Pacific and may even be a prized Scotland-based example from Polmadie sheds. We finally head for home, weary, footsore, grimy but contented. After tea, I open up my Ian Allan abc combined volume and go through my notes for the day, putting crosses where I have seen locos before and a tick where they are new to me. Then I underline my cops very carefully in the com' vol' in red biro and take pleasure from creating runs of consecutive numbers. With everything in its place, I go down to the park and play football with my friends until it goes dark.

I know I risked my life today by not fully having my wits about me whilst crossing busy railway tracks, wandering around industrial sites littered with heavy, angular metal objects protruding from benches and trolleys, crossing the lines between engines slowly rumbling on and off the sheds, skipping over bits of rusty iron partly protruding from the ground, by-passing deep inspection pits, avoiding patches of oil, scalding water running from hoses and piles of red-hot ashes, all with my head buried in a notebook and with half an eye all the time on the lookout for shed staff. Strangely, though, I never feel safer inside than when I am in the company of trains.

Days such as this protect me from my own mediocrity at school, from teachers who criticise rather than encourage, from the relentless competitive jousting involved in making and keeping friends, from the complications and disappointments - the highs and lows - of having a girlfriend, as well as from the threat posed by the local bullies. They are all the growing pains of youth.

My eventual return to Crewe in 2022 looks like its falling into place quite nicely. I will be meeting a Duchess. In fact, we go right back. I'm expecting to renew an acquaintance that has already endured for over sixty years. Coronation Pacific No. 46233 Duchess of Sutherland was based at Edge Hill sheds in Liverpool. Her job was to work the heavy expresses from Lime Street station to London Euston. My job was to go and watch her in action, from time to time. It was there that we first met and we have been the best of friends ever since. She is 11 years older than me but the age gap has never mattered and she is still my number one locomotive.

The Railway Touring Company has obligingly arranged for us to meet again at Crewe on Saturday March 19th. We will share a drink for old time's sake, though it will just be water for her, and I think I'll probably settle for a coffee, just to celebrate. Our rendezvous is set for 11.30 prompt at the end of the platform. I had hoped that she would be wearing dark green, just like in the old days, but I hear that she currently prefers bright red, but I'm happy with that, too.

Sadly, my mid-March date with the Duchess didn't

happen. She cried off at the last minute (and without explanation). I had been stood up. It was obviously not meant to be. Was she out of my class? She was, after all, from the other side of the tracks.

Crewe was just a village when the Grand Junction Railway arrived in 1837. It grew rapidly as part of the London and North Western Railway to become perhaps the best-known railway junction in the world. With a locomotive works, a number of locomotive depots, and services heading off in all directions, including Glasgow, Manchester, Derby, London, Wellington, Birmingham, Shrewsbury, Chester and Liverpool, it became the archetypal railway town. The urban area grew dramatically to serve the railway's needs, and the station became what it still is today - a major location for passengers who need to change trains to reach their eventual destination. The buildings at platform level that date from 1867 have now been awarded Grade II listed status, although the traditional main entrance to Crewe station on Nantwich Road occupies a very cramped site perched on the south side of the railway bridge. Various piecemeal changes have been made to the frontage during the time I've been going there. Most recently, an additional steel and glass entrance has been added round the corner on Weston Road. Expansion on the west side of the current station will provide a hub for HS2. Perhaps these changes will eventually provide a station entrance more befitting of Crewe's strategic importance as a long-established and famous rail centre.

The Manchester independent lines have traditionally been used by freight trains burrowing beneath the West

Coast Main Line north of the station, thus ensuring that they avoid becoming entangled in the comings and goings of passenger trains at the station, itself. As young enthusiasts in the sixties, we knew this line as the Muck Hole. It was legendary amongst spotters and the cry of "Muck Hole" would go up whenever smoke suddenly appeared from southbound traffic as it left the tunnel. Seen from the platforms, the tops of northbound trains had no sooner arrived into view before they, too, dropped down into the abyss. Muck Hole was a very suitable name for it. Smoke continued to drift out of the tunnel portals for some minutes after a train had gone through. For spotters, a decent view could only be gained by trespassing at the bottom of the footbridge provided for railwaymen accessing Crewe North sheds. It was supposedly out of bounds to us. Occasionally, those of us who were brave enough to hang around next to the bottom of the bridge would relay the identity of the latest Muck Hole candidate to those assembled on the platforms. Often, though, Muck Hole-bound locomotives passed through without divulging their identities. As most freight was hauled by less glamorous locomotive classes and because there was usually something more interesting happening on the station itself, the Muck Hole was ignored for a lot of the time, so the cursory shout of "Muck Hole" usually just acknowledged the passing of another number that we had all missed noting. The good news is that it's still there and in use today – it's just not quite so mucky.

We now learn that the Manchester independent lines will not be the only rail tunnel under Crewe in future.

Recently published plans for HS2b, which is intended to take the high-speed railway north of the town as far as Manchester and with a spur to the WCML, just south of Wigan, involve a new south to north tunnel alignment beneath and on the east side of the present station and running parallel to the existing main line.

Exactly a week later, I'm back on track and heading for Crewe. Today, I've already decided, is all yellow - laburnum, daffodils, dandelions, brimstone butterflies and high-vis' cyclists. Ex-GWR Castle Class No. 7027 Clun Castle is doing the honours for steam today and due through at 13.43. The AA Route Planner suggested it would take me one hour and six minutes from home to Uttoxeter station, so an unhurried start from home for the 11.11 departure, a journey timed at 52 minutes for an off-peak return costing £7.30. Buying my ticket at the machine, I'm approached by a man warning me that my chances of getting exactly what I'm expecting from it are remote. I'm taking it one step at a time, while he empties multiple fast-food wrappers into the adjacent waste bin, a task that takes him at least three return visits to his car. I receive the benefit of his advice on each occasion, though I could concentrate better without interruption.

The North Staffordshire Railway station at Uttoxeter dates from 1881, when it replaced the 3 other stations that had served the town previously. The station buildings were destroyed by fire in 1987, leaving it unstaffed thereafter and a predicably somewhat soulless affair with modern shelters on both platforms, relieved only by a semaphore home signal and a good view of the racecourse from the top of the footbridge between the platforms and of the well-wooded ridge behind it.

There are no longer any rules for testing for Covid when re-entering Britain, since I took my trip to Nuneaton. These were the very last conditions to go in England. They have coincided with a dramatic increase in infection rates throughout Britain, due to the latest Omicron variant, BA.2. This appears to be more transmissible but no more severe, though hospital admissions are also up again.

The journey is a mixture of green vales and winding brooks, either side of the sprawling Potteries conurbation. Between Stoke and Kidsgrove - and just to taunt me - the stations and lineside are well-populated with enthusiasts of all ages who are waiting to see the Duchess of Sutherland, no less, fully recovered from whatever caused her "no show" a week ago, and due to follow us on the same track a few minutes later, on her way to Manchester.

Crewe station is heaving. It is doing what Crewe station is there to do - welcoming folk debarking from trains, accommodating them for a short time and packing them off towards their eventual destination. The platform markings implore you to "Stay safe, Stay apart" but there is little chance of that today. Station staff are actually bellowing at travellers to stand behind the yellow line. An announcement claims that a Manchester-bound train is 30 minutes late "because of over-crowding" and suggests that, if your ticket allows you to do so, you should consider taking an alternative train. I walk across the bridge to the most westerly platform, number 12, where Clun Castle is due to be pathed. It is an oasis of calm, compared to 5 and 6, which are both being used bidirectionally, as required. I have a bit of a wander around to reacquaint myself with the lie of the land. I'm struck with the amount of land the railways used at Crewe in the past that is not being used today, but which could be brought back into service with HS2 in mind. I eat my sandwich and crisps on one of the now very infrequently provided seating areas, keeping my bag close to my feet so that it is not swept up as unaccounted for and summarily "destroyed or damaged by the security services". Clun Castle puts in her brief appearance and she is bang on time.

She glides effortlessly through the station and round the curve towards Chester. She is resplendent, but the event is short-lived, very quiet and curiously low key, with only a smattering of fans at the platform end to pay tribute to her. At least I made the effort, I thought, as I turned for home. I comforted myself with the thought that we are both still here, and that hopefully we will meet again soon.

13. Llangollen

You can't beat a lads' day out for a bit of bonhomie and banter. In October 2016, we took an away day at the Llangollen Railway's Autumn Steam Gala. Little did we know that the LR would soon become embroiled in financial difficulties which would threaten its very existence. It precipitated persistently for most of the day we were there, but it takes more than a spot of rain to dampen the spirits when we all get together.

If there was ever a case for an over-all cab roof, then that wet day was it, but the Gala's visiting engine was the former Lancashire and Yorkshire Railway Aspinall Class 27 No. 1300 from the East Lancashire Railway, and she was not so blessed in that department. Built in Horwich in 1896, and withdrawn from service in 1960, she is the only surviving example from a class that once numbered 484 engines, of which I managed to see just 6. They were the L&YR's standard goods locomotives.

We soon discovered that the planned guided tours of the workshops were all booked up for the day. Brief but intense negotiations followed, resulting in an extra tour being laid on just for us. Pamphlets and information boards can't compete with first-hand descriptions straight from the horse's mouth, so we were all riveted - figuratively, that is.

The scenic Dee valley route is possibly unsurpassed in that respect on any of our heritage railways and it is soon to be re-opened to Corwen. We had hoped it would be completed by the time of our next visit, but we'll just have to come again. Our train from Llangollen to Carrog in 2016 had been hauled by the then resident ex-GWR Manor Class No. 7822 Foxcote Manor. We could remember seeing her at the end of her time on BR - withdrawn from service, cold and neglected in the sidings at Shrewsbury shed, in December 1965.

The cosy cafe at Berwyn station beckoned and we ended the day doing what we do best these days - sitting around having a laugh over a nice cup of tea and a scone, whilst churning out the memories from the more than half a century of friendship that has elapsed since we first all got together. My friend Andy told me when we were youngsters that I would write a book about cafes one day, such was the affection I must have shown for dropping in on them. In those days, that included milk bars and Wimpy burger bars. There was one of those next to the entrance to Liverpool Lime Street station that I certainly frequented. Milk bars in some of the North Wales towns were within easy reach on a day trip from the Wirral by car in the late 60s. They were characterised by Formica surfaces, sticky oil-cloth table coverings, a pinball machine or a juke box, a curvy sign or two of neon lights, an overwhelming aroma of deep-fried food and permanently misted-up windows.

As young train spotters, station buffets sometimes offered us refuge from poor weather. I temporarily retreated from cold and biting winds at Chester General and Crewe, from freezing fog in Selby, from scorching sun at Exeter St David's, and more recently I found sanctuary from heavy rain in the station café at Bolton Abbey, the re-built terminus of the heritage railway line from Embsay.

They were always welcoming, with a hiss from the tea urn, a whiff of hot sausage rolls from the kitchen and that smoky atmosphere to peer through that we didn't mind at all at the time, but which I would immediately turn my back on today. Generally lowered tones from passengers in transit contrasted with the intermittent volleys of laughter and more business-like exchanges from those on the other side of the counter.

The most famous of all such locations is surely at Carnforth. Returning from a holiday in the Lake District, we made a point of checking out the excellent station museum and enjoyed a very tasty snack at a reasonable price and a giant pot of tea to go with it. A trio of smartly dressed women arrived in the doorway - young professionals, complete with overnight cases, lap-tops and various other bits of hand luggage. Working out that they could fit in a brief sit down before taking their train south to join a London connection at Lancaster, the leading lady paused briefly on the threshold before they all spilled into the café for afternoon tea. "Ooh, look.... It's just like something out of .... (pondering for another second or two) .... Brief Encounter!"

My only gripe with the heritage centre and the café at Carnforth was that it shut at 4.00 p.m. and we had been caught out by this on an earlier return trip from the north. I thought that this closing halfway through the afternoon lark was a thing of the past. Why did the change of heart that deregulated pub closing times and facilitated Sunday shop opening never work through to coaxing café proprietors to adjust their opening hours with the more flexible requirements of the present century in mind?

While we are on the point, our local leisure centre is closed on bank holidays. Isn't that simply a contradiction in terms? Anyway, its baffling to me that the very time that you might want a nice cup of tea and a bite to eat after a pleasant afternoon walk in spring or summer coincides with the moment that they draw down the shutters or turn round that little open/closed notice that hangs between the lace curtain and the glass panel in the door.

It does make sense that for heritage railway cafes there will be a coincidence between closing time and the completed running of the last train of the day - though please don't rush it. Town centre locations have no such excuse. October 2009 found us in Kingsbridge in Devon, since 1963 unfortunately no longer connected to the ex-GWR Paddington to Penzance line at South Brent. At around 4.00 we were predictably met with the greeting that "The kitchen is closed now, but you can have a cup of tea". Even that was better than the day before in Bigbury (nearest station Ivybridge, on the main line east of Plymouth), where the café was simply closed all day – in half term week!

At a café on the main street in Beaumaris on the island of Anglesey (5 miles from Bangor railway station, but never, apparently, itself rail connected), a twee, olde worlde affair where the waitresses still wore Victorian-style frilly aprons and there were too many chairs and tables for you to feel quite comfortable, with your arms firmly tucked in by your side in case you nudged someone accidentally on the next table, a mother asked, "Could you do small omelettes for the children, please?" The waitress with the white headband thought for a second and shook her head. She walked off. She came back. "We can do a 2-egg instead of a 3-egg, but it will still be big". The family agreed on an omelette to share. I picked my head up off the table. The café has a newspaper article on the wall to let customers know that the Hairy Bikers had once stopped by. I wondered if they had felt a bit hemmed in and how well they had coped with the big omelette.

Coffee at coffee bars came as an instant powder of unknown origin from the depths of an industrial-sized paint tin. It was then further damaged by having scalding water poured over it. Sandwiches were usually of sliced white bread, and lettuce had not yet given birth to baby leaf salad. Progress has not always been totally reassuring, however. I picked up a packet of crisps not long ago which claimed that it was roasted chicken and thyme flavoured and made with real ingredients. Well, fancy that.

At a café in Pwllheli, joyfully still rail linked at the northern extremity of the ex-GWR line around Cardigan Bay and which we reached from Machynlleth in August 2010 behind Stanier Class Five No. 44871, I asked for a tuna and mayonnaise sandwich without butter. My logic was that there is already enough fat in the sandwich with the mayo, thank you. I don't need another splodge of margarine as well. This request so perturbed the "cook", that rather than handing it over to the waitress to deliver it, he emerged from the kitchen to see what sort of fussy creature had dared to ask for something so wayward from his usual unreconstructed fare. "You're still going to die, you know", he announced to the room, as he slid the plate in my general direction. Welcome to Wales, I thought, though his Scouse accent was actually stronger than mine.

In Llangrannog, a pretty seaside location but unfortunately a full 22 miles from Carmarthen railway station and even further from the railhead at Aberystwyth, we were told, "There is no soup. It's 5.00 o'clock, we've stopped serving food, there's only scones and biscuits". We gave them a miss on the grounds that having just about digested the logic, a reasoned response might not have been welcomed. A friend told me about a café where they would not serve her a teacake in the afternoon. She had been told that it was "Mornings only, for teacakes".

In 2009, the Guardian named the ten best railway cafes in Britain. I think they were, more strictly, the result of some nominations by fairly well-known local people, so less of an objective assessment and more a bit of light-hearted promotion. Carnforth and Worksop (both of which I can vouch for) made the list, as did Kyle of Lochalsh, Woodbridge, Grindleford, St Erth, Manningtree, Wymondham, Huddersfield and Barnstaple. My own recommendations would include Bodmin Road, where the signal box at the junction station on the ex-GWR main line and the Bodmin and Wenford Railway has become a much publicised and award-winning eating establishment, as well as the fabulous modern complexes at King's Cross and St Pancras, where, in the case of the latter, a whole host of units fill the spaces in the glass-fronted ground floor archways. Great Malvern has a lovely café in a well-preserved station, which is especially noteworthy for its restored decorative iron work. At Newark Northgate, Chris's favourite chain provided a splendid coffee as the prelude for Bittern's 92 mph run through in 2013, and the old station building at Alnwick, now occupied by Barter Books, the famous second-hand bookshop (and buffet), is simply a wonder to behold.

Back at Berwyn, enthusiastic and friendly volunteers run the authentic station café, surrounded by suitable prints and posters from the middle of the last century, but one is still spoilt for choice, because on the other side of the Chain Bridge over the River Dee, the hotel has recently been renovated and from its river-side terrace, customers have a great view of the action on the railway.

En route to my son's wedding in Brighton in 2010, the "Rail Gourmet" employee had not turned up for his shift. There was no buffet in standard class all the way to St Pancras. The guard/ticket collector/conductor/train announcer/attendant/sometime cabaret artist, who was called Tim, said he would "break gourmet bloke's legs next time he saw him". Tim was then straight into his other tasks. "We apologise for the fact that there is no coach B. This is because of a fatality earlier in the week". Too much information, Tim. Maybe he was still seething about the extra hassle that Gourmet Bloke had set him up for, but Tim was only just getting into his stride. "Bags do not have a ticket, but fare-paying passengers do". He left it at that, "So move them", being the implied directive. "The next station will be

Wellingborough……(short pause)….no it won't. That would be a small miracle as we have just left there. The next station will be Bedford". And, finally, "We are currently running four minutes late due to the volume of passengers boarding and disembarking from the train". Well it must have really taken them by surprise, that one, having passengers in some numbers to deal with.

By now I had realised that for budding entertainers, the onboard PA system provides young comedians with their first real gig before a captive audience. You can't just walk out at half time, as I had done from the Phillip Glass Ensemble's concert in Bristol, having attended for the first few "numbers" at someone else's invitation. I also walked out of "Cats" in Nottingham half way through and made straight for the bar. Whilst we were in Brighton, or rather, in "Hove, Actually", as the more upwardly mobile residents prefer to call it, a couple of notices caught my eye. The first was on the side of a mobile fish and chip van, which read, "No fish and chips are left in this van overnight" and just down the road was a large wheelie bin, with a rather ominous warning on the side, "Do not sleep in this bin". That left us with the over-night and evening meal still to sort out and without any obvious pointers for breakfast, either.

Before getting back to Llangollen, Chris and I had spent mid-April in 2022 visiting our son and his family in the United States. If Covid rules had by then evaporated for the UK, there was certainly still a lot to consider before stepping on a plane to the States. This included travel tickets that were transferable if Covid struck in an untimely fashion, personal

insurance that covered Coronavirus infection, Covid
vaccination passports especially for travel, a viral antigen test
taken within one day of our planned departure and a
printable seven-page signed attestation form to that effect
allowing entry to the USA - plus compulsory mask wearing on
the plane and at International Airport Dulles, Washington DC,
on arrival. Not quite over then, at least as far as America was
concerned.

The first railway station at Llangollen was opened by the
Vale of Llangollen Railway in 1862 as the terminus of the line
from the junction at Ruabon. Three years later, the separate
Langollen and Corwen Railway took the line further west and
at the same time opened the current station in a more
central location within the town. The completed route to
Barmouth on the coast of Cardigan Bay was via the shores of
Lake Bala and the former county town of Merionethshire at
Dolgellau, where it joined up with the Cambrian Railway. The

whole route eventually became part of the Great Western Railway. BR closed the line for passengers in 1965 and for freight in 1968. It has been reopened in stages as a heritage railway from 1981.

On 28th April 2022, a group of holiday makers from Pennsylvania enjoyed the journey with us up the valley from Llangollen in the two-car DMU. Their Liverpudlian tour guide was gamely endeavouring to pronounce appropriately the names of some of the places in the area. I think in his position, I might have stuck to rocks and history.

Carrog station is a delight, with its own cosy café and extra picnic benches on the platform. Rebuilt by Llangollen Railway volunteers, the station is set in an attractive, hilly landscape laced with patches of woodland. The Covid notice on the platform politely asked visitors to respect other peoples' personal space, and on the day, there was plenty of personal space available. Face coverings were optional but recommended and the tone of the messaging was by now all very subdued. The seventeenth century stone bridge over the Dee led us to the Grouse Inn for a hearty lunch.

The Llangollen Railway has visibly suffered from its serious setbacks in recent times, but it would be no surprise to me, if, a few years from now, the level of provision we had previously become used to here had been restored again in its entirety. To its credit, the railway preservation movement has recorded many more victories than defeats over recent decades and will, no doubt, continue to do so.

14. Back Down to Earth

So, what of the pandemic, at the end of April 2022? Initially, the threat posed by this unknown disease was daunting, if not terrifying. When I began to put this account together in the middle of 2021, it was still the dominant issue each day in news broadcasts and the press. It faded from this prominent position very quickly in 2022, as Omicron failed to pose the same intensity of problems as the previous variants. Nevertheless, we should avoid complacency, as further and more damaging mutations are always a possibility.

Two years was a lot of time devoted to keeping Covid at arms' length, but that is what we resolved to do from the outset - follow the rules and have our own extra ones if we thought the decision makers had got it wrong. I had faith from the start that science would prevail. I told my daughters that we would be OK if we were patient and cautious. Pandemics through history have been things that come, do their worst, then go. We just had to see it out. Humanity is extraordinary in meeting challenges and devising technological breakthroughs when required. I know I have been on the cautious side of average, which probably just reflects the way I am. I know people who have been much more cavalier than we have and those who have been more wary. There is a balance to be struck and that risk has to be set alongside all the other things that can get you. Future scrutiny will conclude as to how our leaders performed overall, but it seemed that the time taken to introduce appropriate interventions early on was often woeful. When the science was blatantly screaming for action, the government hesitated and delayed and that must have been very costly, health-wise. The eventual lifting of restrictions seemed more sure-footed. The vaccination programme was a major success, for which the authorities deserve credit in quickly going for a mass vaccination programme and for securing the necessary drugs. The greatest credit, however, goes to the scientists who developed the vaccines and to the NHS who applied them and who have responded so valiantly throughout to the horrors of the pandemic, face-to-face. I'm only too well aware that many others have been much more directly affected by Covid than us and we have frequently been saddened by reports about those families that have really suffered.

The other big issue that has helped sweep Covid from our day-to-day consciousness has been the Russian invasion of Ukraine. It is another stark reminder of how threats to well-being can suddenly appear as if from nowhere, or so it seems. It is with an acute awareness of the bravery and resilience of the people of Ukraine that I end these relatively frivolous attempts to find pleasant diversions on the uneven path through life. Until a few weeks ago, I had naively thought that the legacy left to us by our parents' generation was to have put an end to old-fashioned territorial wars in Europe. I am devoting this book to my grandchildren, in the hope that they find peace, love - including a love of place - and the contentment that comes from the pursuit of simple pleasures.

Gratefully, we are now fully back on track. I'm looking forward to walking along the headland from Hope Cove to

Bolt Tail in South Devon again, and to gazing south from the summit of Latrigg over a tranquil Derwentwater towards England's highest mountains. In railway terms, an overnight on the Caledonian sleeper from Euston to Inverness certainly appeals and yet another return to Bewdley – a favourite station and a regular "must" for the last few hours of a four-day Severn Valley Railway gala - later on the Sunday afternoon when most of the punters have left but the locos haven't yet been put to bed.

We went to the pub to celebrate a recent birthday. Choosing an appropriate card had taken some time, as the birthday boy has a dry sense of humour. We plumped for one based on a cartoon from a well-known satirical magazine that had made me laugh out loud in the shop. It made the recipient laugh out loud when he first saw it, too, but that had been a long time ago. Though our endeavours had fallen flat, I was consoled by comments that it had been a "nice try". The conversation turned briefly to my blog. Someone observed that "It's all about trains". "I know, I'm sorry about that", was as much as I could offer on the spur of the moment, in response to the obvious disappointment that I'd caused. It is essentially, of course, a railway blog. My cunning plan was to promote our rich railway heritage by trying to entertain those who already have an interest, and at the same time by bringing it to the attention of those who don't. I'm not sure how to address success or failure in this quest, but I'm amusing myself and it keeps me off the streets, though more exercise on the streets may actually be more beneficial to me in the longer term. I do have a less frivolous and less self-indulgent side, but I don't think that the audience I'm aiming for would wish me to bang on about things that I very definitely have opinions on, although every now and then I just can't help myself. I want it to be an overall positive experience. I want to rejoice in what has been achieved so far by the preservation movement and to advocate the case for further action in terms of conservation. I want to celebrate how other people pursue their railway-related interests and to communicate the enjoyment I've had at the line-side and pretty much everywhere else.

Will I be able to share my love of place with my grandchildren - that panorama of sea, islands and mountains from the (not very high) highest point on Iona, the lights of the Liverpool waterfront at night from the promenade "over the water", lively seas and green serpentine cliffs hemming in the coves on the Lizard, an exhilarating romp down the springy turf of Fairfield overlooking Morecambe Bay, a stroll down to Waverley station from the Royal Mile in Edinburgh at dusk as the lights come on along Princes Street, or up close and noisy (and smelly) at our amazing seabird colonies - Bempton cliffs or the Farne Islands by small boat from Seahouses? Maybe not, but that's fine. I'm confident that eventually they will all find their own places to love.

I had a window seat facing the Arctic on our way back from America. Following the eastern seaboard, it takes the best part of three hours out of Washington to eventually leave that continent behind and head out from Newfoundland over the Atlantic. I could see little at all from my window seat until a deep red glow suddenly appeared on the horizon to herald the dawning of the next day. I played with my interactive seatback flight path map – just as interesting as any of the media offerings designed to side-track me. Our tiny group of islands crept into view on the right of my screen. What fascinating shapes they are – cut adrift from the European mainland but so obviously connected to it by the continental shelf. Britain's attractive and intriguingly indented coastline leaning forward over the smaller island to the west, perched as they both are on the brink of the ocean deep. The first visible sign of settlement from 41,000 feet up was provided by the street lights of Limerick. What riches there are down there between here and Heathrow, I thought, as the light grew brighter and the shortest of sleepless nights gave way to daylight. A carpet of cloud promptly cut off the Irish Sea, Pembrokeshire's wonderful (and comparatively underpopulated) beaches, the Forest of Dean, the River Wye and the beautiful city of Bath, beneath, but I could see them all in my mind's eye and each one brought back memories from different times – dipping my toes in freezing seawater on the pristine sands at Marloes, watching the nesting peregrines at Symond's Yat, chatting with two octogenarian former coal miners with the strongest possible local accents in a Parkend pub in Dennis Potter-land, where the sheep still had right of way on the street outside, and admiring the elegant Georgian buildings of the Roman spa city, from the Royal Crescent to the façade of (Victorian) Green Park station - that constant reminder of the old Somerset and Dorset Joint Railway. How lucky we are to have all this to choose from - and so much more.